The History of Silver Lake

As Told Through Its Deeds

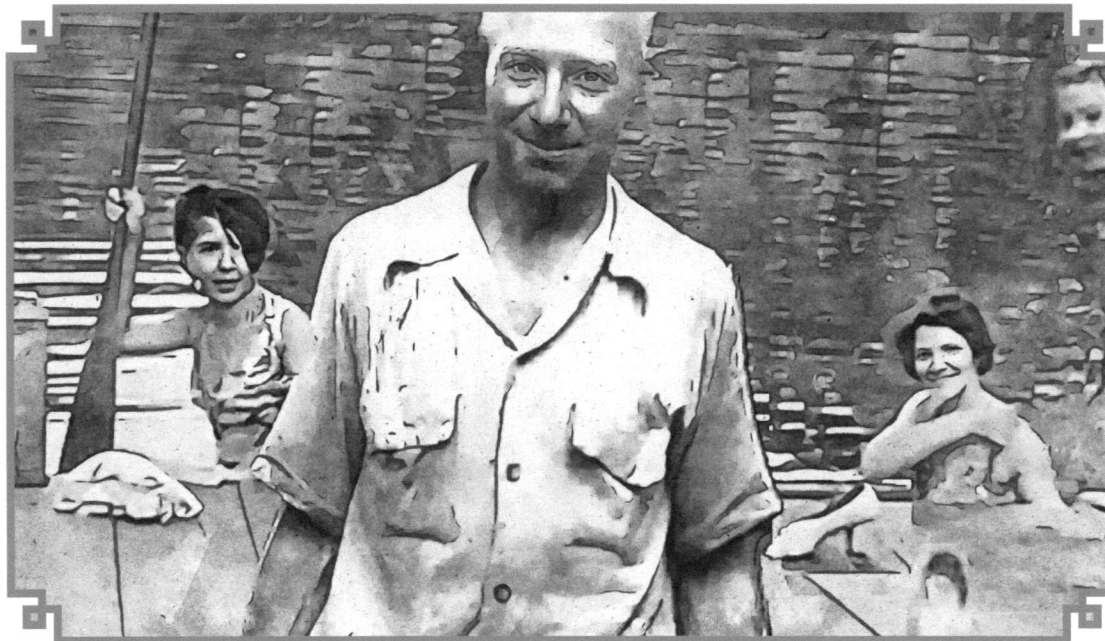

Scott and Kathleen Webb

For more information, including bulk ordering, visit us on the internet at HistoryofSilverLake.com

Edited by Lil Barcaski

Published by: GWN Publishing, LLC | www.GWNPublishing.com

Cover Design: Kristina Conatser | www.capturedbykcdesigns.com

Paperback ISBN: 978-1-959608-74-5

Hardcover ISBN: 978-1-959608-75-2

To our mothers, Barb and Anne, whose wisdom saw the love we had yet to perceive, guiding us to a joyful marriage. In their insight, they were wiser than we were smart, not realizing their counsel on matters of the heart.

To our friends and family, both near and far, past, present, and future, who visit, find peace, make memories, and enjoy entertainment with us in our little slice of heaven on Silver Lake.

PREFACE

We are third-generation property owners on Silver Lake, with deep appreciation for the vital role our small lake and its community have played in our family's story. Over its 250-year history, the purpose and function of Silver Lake have undergone significant transformations. As we plan to pass ownership to the next generation, we feel compelled to provide them and the entire lake community with reliable historical information. We hope to assist the next generation to fulfill their future stewardship responsibilities.

So, we embarked on the journey of chronicling the history of Silver Lake. We were surprised to find that no formal account of the lake's centuries-long narrative exists. What we had held to be true was largely based on oral tradition, which had gradually evolved over time. This challenge is not unique to Silver Lake but is a common characteristic of history itself. The facts, as they existed in their own time, are often subject to misinterpretation or misremembering. Looking back more than two centuries, we have discovered and chronicled the evolution of Silver Lake from a functional mill pond to a seasonal summer colony, and eventually to a small permanent year-round community. Nevertheless, we acknowledge the presence of knowledge gaps, which have, at times, required us to make assumptions to bridge them. In these instances, we have taken great care to clearly label these assumptions, ensuring that our readers are aware of areas where improvement and further research are needed.

In the pursuit of truth, hours of exhaustive research have occasionally led to moments of desperation, where the temptation to lean on assumptions to expedite our journey became attractive. It was during these moments that we coined a term adopted from the iconic scene from Jurassic Park where scientists, faced with insufficient "Dino" DNA for cloning, resorted to splicing it with frog DNA, resulting in catastrophic consequences. In our case, "I think you're adding frog DNA," became the gentle reminder between us, as the authors, to return to the sources and keep diligently pursuing accuracy.

Our quest to document the historical record spans the spectrum from seemingly trivial details, such as the origin of Silver Lake's name, to the vital recognition of the lake's original builders and how the 20th Century establishment of the Silver Lake summer colony came about. Equally significant is our endeavor to highlight essential responsibilities and challenges associated with the lake's maintenance, a duty shared by residents, past, present, and future.

Our research revealed a significant insight, exemplified by a 6th-grade class in 1964 whose assignment was to learn about their York County history. Their modest goal was not to create an all-encompassing account, but to present what they had uncovered, in the hope that more fragments of the past could be preserved and utilized in the future. We have endeavored to do the same.

Now, within these pages, we present our findings on Silver Lake, painstakingly researched and documented for posterity. Our aim has been to minimize any "frog DNA" in our account, preserving the history of our cherished community as faithfully as possible.

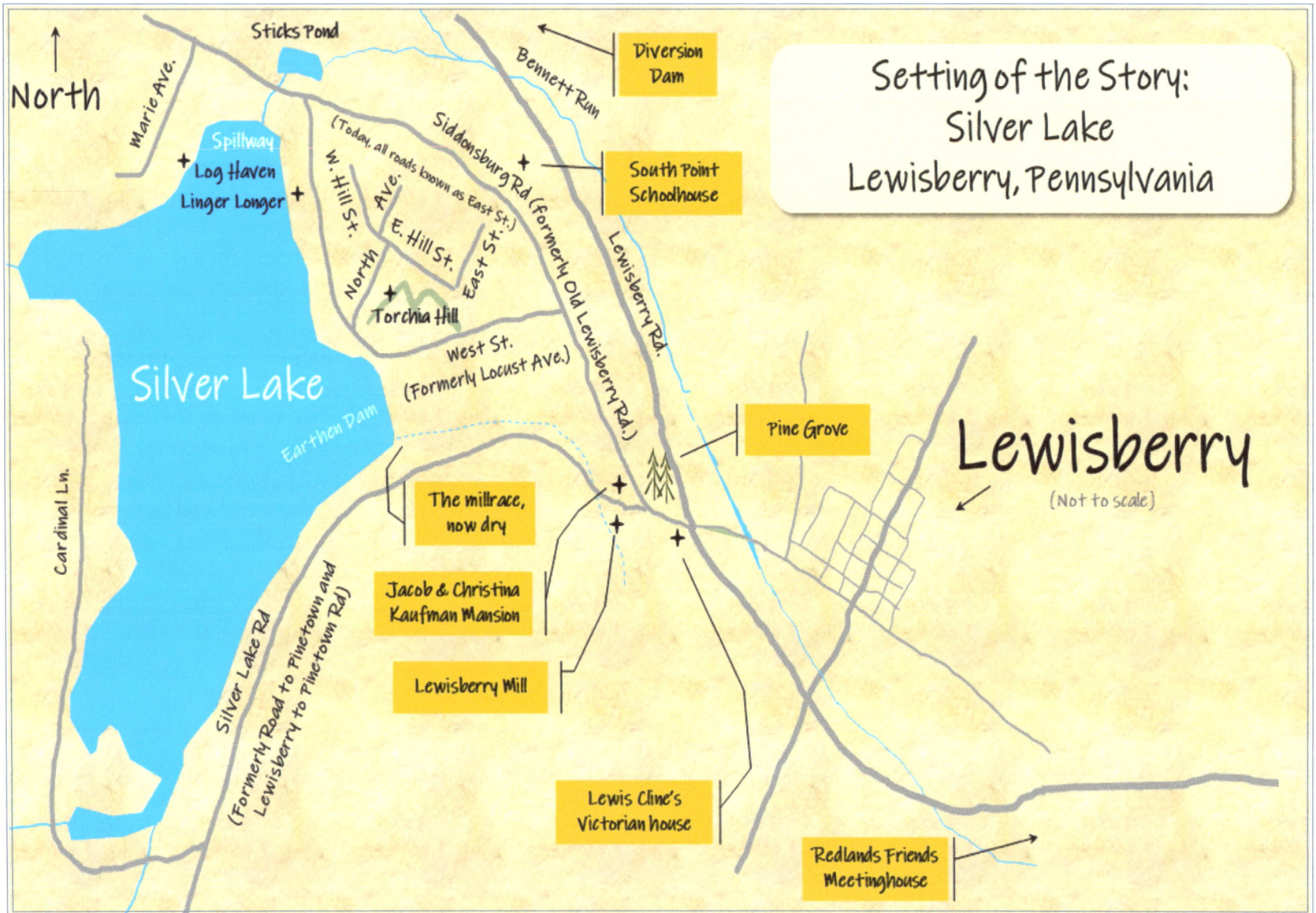

North

Sticks Pond

Marie Ave.

Spillway
Log Haven
Linger Longer

W. Hill St.

North Ave.

E. Hill St.

East St.

(Today, all roads known as East St.)

Siddonsburg Rd

Bennett Run

Diversion Dam

South Point Schoolhouse

Lewisberry Rd. (formerly Old Lewisberry Rd.)

Torchia Hill

West St.
(Formerly Locust Ave.)

Silver Lake

Earthen Dam

Cardinal Ln.

Pine Grove

Lewisberry

(Not to scale)

The millrace, now dry

Jacob & Christina Kaufman Mansion

Lewisberry Mill

Silver Lake Rd
(Formerly Road to Pinetown and Lewisberry to Pinetown Rd)

Lewis Cline's Victorian house

Redlands Friends Meetinghouse

Setting of the Story:
Silver Lake
Lewisberry, Pennsylvania

4

Setting of the Story: Central and Southeast Pennsylvania

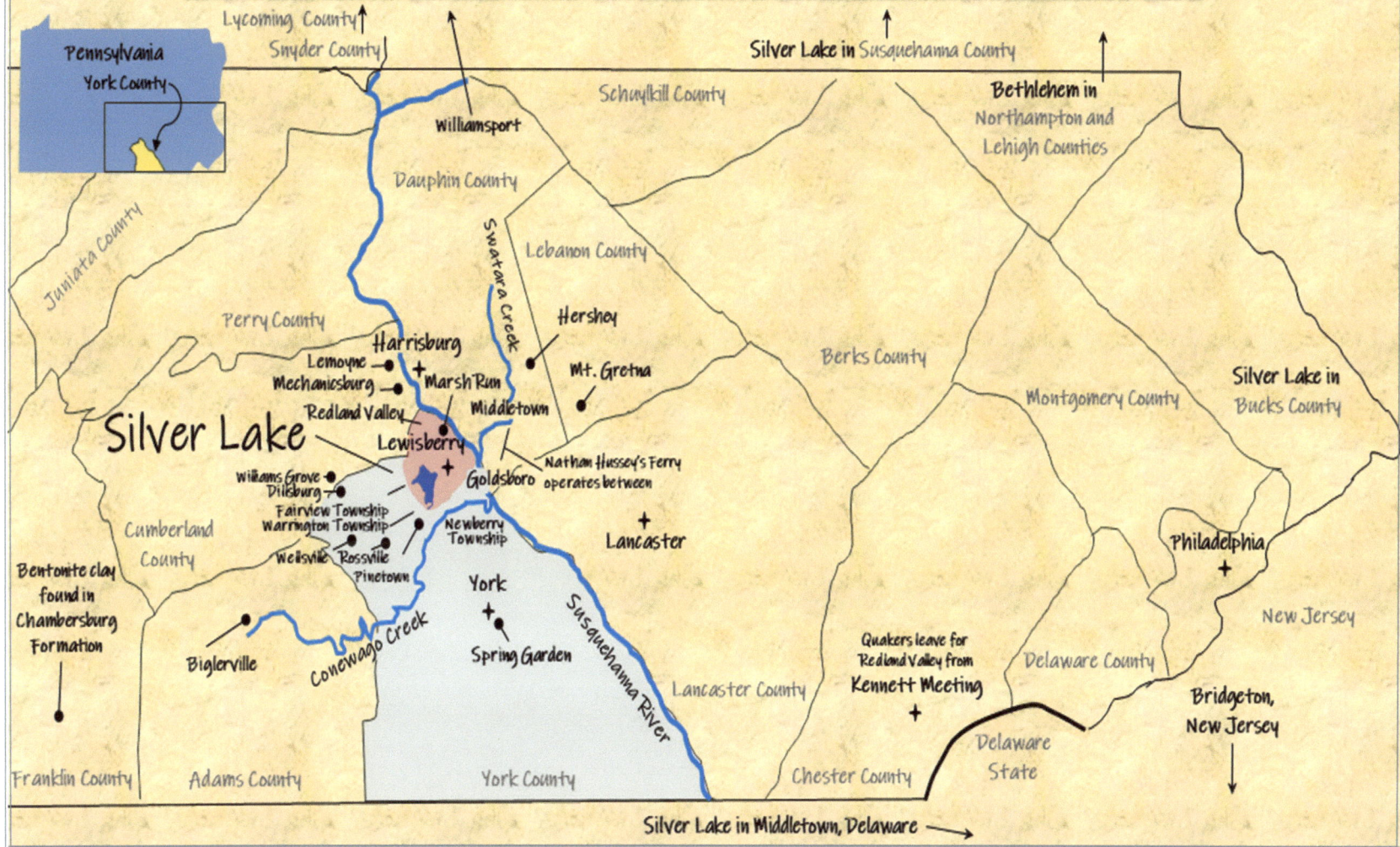

Pennsylvania
York County

Lycoming County
Snyder County
Williamsport

Silver Lake in Susquehanna County

Schuylkill County

Bethlehem in Northampton and Lehigh Counties

Juniata County

Dauphin County

Swatara Creek

Lebanon County

Perry County

Hershey

Harrisburg
Lemoyne
Mechanicsburg
Marsh Run
Redland Valley
Mt. Gretna
Middletown

Berks County

Montgomery County

Silver Lake in Bucks County

Silver Lake

Lewisberry
Williams Grove
Dillsburg
Fairview Township
Warrington Township
Wellsville   Rossville
Pinetown

Goldsboro
Nathan Hussey's Ferry operates between
Newberry Township

Lancaster

Philadelphia

Cumberland County

New Jersey

Bentonite clay found in Chambersburg Formation

Biglerville

Conewago Creek

York
Spring Garden

Susquehanna River

Quakers leave for Redland Valley from Kennett Meeting

Delaware County

Bridgeton, New Jersey

Lancaster County

Delaware State

Franklin County

Adams County

York County

Chester County

Silver Lake in Middletown, Delaware →

CONTENTS

INTRODUCTION

Geographical Forces at Work: A Mill Pond Emerges

A short distance from the historic town of Lewisberry Pennsylvania, York County's Silver Lake holds both an interesting history and natural beauty. This modest 22-acre water body may, at first glance, appear unpretentious, but its 250-year history tells the story of the evolution of Central Pennsylvania. Once an essential mill pond, it played a pivotal role in the lives of numerous mill owners, most notably the Cline family, and the farming community the mill supported. It was during the stewardship of Lewis Cline, when the name Silver Lake first appears, that the mill pond began its transformation into a desirable recreational destination.

Situated within the Gettysburg Formation, a specific rock unit within the broader Gettysburg-Newark Lowland Section, Silver Lake finds itself in a region characterized by undulating low hills and valleys adorned with striking red sedimentary rock.[1,2]

The origin of Silver Lake is set against a backdrop of ancient rifts, tracing their origins back to the breakup of the supercontinent Pangaea. Left behind were narrow river valleys and basins. The environment was similar to that of today's Floridian Everglades including reptiles, amphibians. and dinosaurs. The Gettysburg Formation, dating to the Late Triassic Period, primarily comprises reddish sandstone and shale, with a minor presence of conglomerate. The Gettysburg conglomerate[3] borders the eastern side of Silver Lake.

With elevations that range from 20 to 1,355 feet, it includes landmarks locally referred to as Pinetown Hill, Wrights Knob, and Moores Mountain. Higher elevations are underlain with an igneous rock known as diabase. Diabase, formerly magma, appeared in the Jurassic period and healed fissures

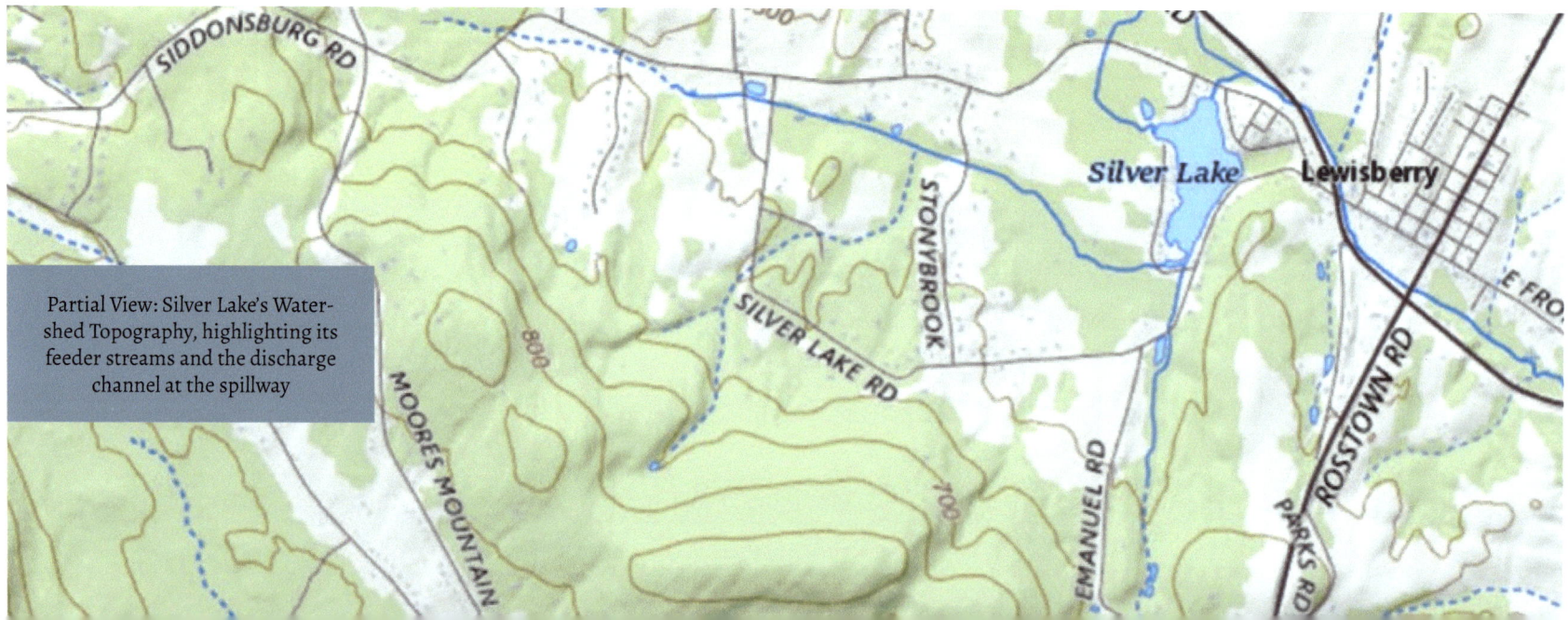

Partial View: Silver Lake's Watershed Topography, highlighting its feeder streams and the discharge channel at the spillway

caused by Pangean breakup. It's worth noting that the natural gap and gradual incline at Emanuel Road served as an ideal east-west route for travelers between Lewisberry and Pinetown in the 19th Century. Rivers and streams meander through this terrain, influencing both its physical form and its functional role in the region.[4]

In its natural state, the area of Silver Lake was a modest duck pond, primarily fed by two streams and a few underground springs. Water levels would fluctuate, rising during periods of abundant rainfall and receding during droughts. The transformation of the natural wetlands into a functional mill pond was achieved by adding two dams and a third diversion dam, which redirected water from the Bennett Run stream through a hand-dug diversion channel or race—now recognized as a feeder stream. This adaptation allowed the mill pond to store and release water, harnessing it as an energy source to power the downstream mill.

Mills played a crucial role for the early Pennsylvania settlers, enabling them to grind grain they raised into grist or meal

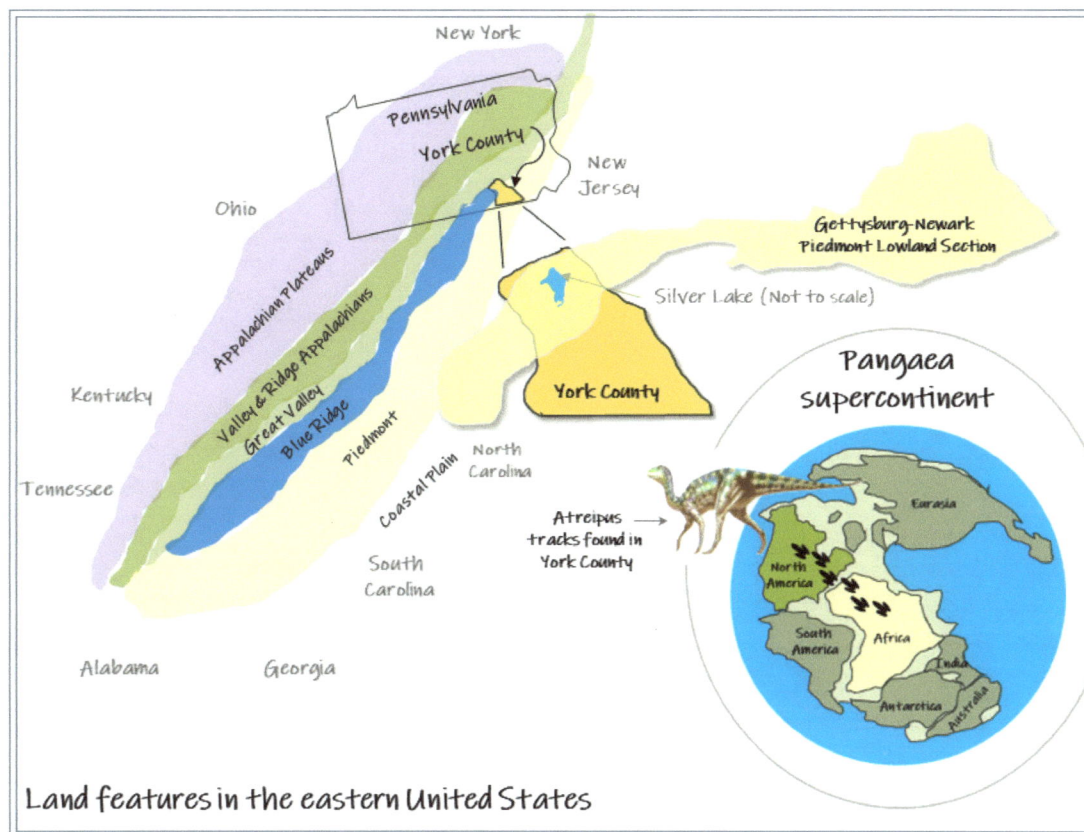

Geological Forces at Work – A Mill Pond Emerges (Authors' Illustration)

for culinary uses, as well as to rough-cut logs into planks for various purposes.

As Pennsylvania colonists ventured westward across the Susquehanna River in the 18th century, the local land surrounding Silver Lake gained value, and a story traceable through the deeds can be told. These deeds, along with the genealogy of the land's proprietors, the results of the decisions they made, and their personal narratives, come together to form a tale that is typical of the region.

Mixed Flock of Ducks (Courtesy of Ken Boyer)

THE FIRST EUROPEAN SETTLERS ARRIVE

Innovative Crossing: Ellis Lewis and Quakers Use Canoes to Transport Horses
Across the Susquehanna (Authors' illustration)

THE FIRST EUROPEAN SETTLERS ARRIVE

Agroup of adventurous English Quakers embarked on a journey in the mid-18th century that would shape the landscape and spirit of a new frontier – the Redland Valley. Ellis Lewis, John Rankin, James Bennett, and a small Quaker community relocated here from Kennett Meeting, Chester County, Pennsylvania in approximately 1734. [5] The first official land grants west of the Susquehanna were recorded in 1741.

The Redland Valley Quaker community grew, influenced the region's development, and generally lived peacefully with the indigenous Susquehannock people, who had been much diminished by strife with the Seneca tribe. Quakers, with their guiding principles of non-violence, belief that God lives in all souls and therefor all life is sacred, as well as the obligations of stewardship, were uniquely able to develop peaceful relationships with the indigenous peoples. They established a

" *Some of the English Quakers crossed the Susquehanna here as early as 1734. Five years later, a temporary road was opened on the York County side. Thomas Hall, John McFesson, Joseph Bennett, John Heald, John Rankin, and Ellis Lewis from Chester County, crossed the Susquehanna from the mouth of the Swatara, and selected lands on the west side of the river in the year 1734. It has often been related of them, that when they arrived on the eastern bank of the river, and there being no other kinds of crafts than canoes to cross, they fastened two together, and placed their horses' front feet in one canoe and the hind feet in another, then piloted the frail crafts, with their precious burden, across the stream by means of poles. The ferry obtained its present name, and was licensed in 1790.* [6] "

Middletown Ferry

string of communities in present-day Newberry, Fairview, and Warrington Townships. The fertile lands and Susquehanna River continued to attract more settlers, contributing to Redland Valley's expansion and heritage.

English Quaker settlers largely established north of Conewago Creek. They typically migrated from Chester and Lancaster Counties to present-day York County via the bustling gateway that was Nathan Hussey's Ferry, which ran between Middletown and Goldsboro.[7] Ferry service was established in 1738 and most migrants from Lancaster traveled this way. The Redland Valley and Lewisberry were among the first Quaker settlements in America west of the Susquehanna River.[8] Embracing the beauty of the land, they nurtured their vibrant culture and, with hard work and ingenuity, prospered.

A land grant, dated June 20, 1741, to William Passmore marks the earliest documented instance of land ownership encompassing the area with Silver Lake. This grant was issued for

lands in present-day Newberry, Fairview, Warrington, and Monaghan Townships by Pennsylvania's Provincial Governors—John Penn, Thomas Penn, and Richard Penn—sons and heirs of William Penn, the founder of the Province of Pennsylvania.

Harmon Updegraff received a land patent from William Passmore, recorded in Philadelphia on July 5, 1765, encompassing a portion of Mr. Passmore's land that incorporates Silver Lake. Updegraff was a tanner and shoemaker by occupation.[9]

An excerpt from the Updegraff to Harmon deed, shown below, outlines the chain of title for the land that Herman Updegraff is preparing to convey to John Harmon—from the provincial governors to William Passmore, then to Herman Updegraff, and finally to John Harmon.[10]

Quaker pioneers continued to shape the landscape in the Redland Valley throughout the 18th Century. Rough roads were cut, land cleared

Historical Chain of Title: From Provincial Governors to John Harmon, as Documented in the Updegraff: Harmon Deed

Mason's Mark on the John and Elizabeth Harmon brownstone mill (Authors' Photograph)

for farming, and small communities established. The land that includes present day Silver Lake, 422 acres, was purchased by another Quaker pioneer, John Harmon/Herman, from Harmon Updegraff in 1781.

Mr. Harmon proceeded to build a grist mill, which was operational by 1786. The mill structure and the miller's home still stand today on the outskirts of the borough of Lewisberry. To power this mill he labored to create a viable mill pond by utilizing the nearby water-rich wetlands, located about a quarter mile to

the west and with a 15-foot elevation difference. The features Harmon constructed included a hand-dug diversion channel—also documented as a mill race—from Bennett Run (a tributary of Conewago Creek) to fill Silver Lake. Additionally, there was an earthen dam and an earthen race connecting the lake to the mill. Remnants of the race still exist, while the earthen dam remains intact and functional to this day.

The inscription on the cornerstone of John Harman's mill roughly translates as "Samuel Knisley Mason John Harmon and Elizabeth his wife October 1785 in the 10th year of American Independence".

The mill underwent several name changes over its operational history—initially known as Harmon's Mill, then renamed Kaufman's Mill, followed by Clines' Mill. Through these various name changes, it eventually became referred to as Lewisberry Mills.[11]

The Harmon family sold the mill and surrounding lands to John and Magdelena Kaufman in 1797.[12] Interestingly, the Harmon to Kaufman transfer is the first mention of water rights from the Bennett Run diversion channel. This statement in the deed would prove instrumental to the survival of Silver Lake more than 150 years later.

The mill remained in the hands of the Kaufman family for a half century. John Kaufman sold to Jacob Kaufman, presumably a family member, and his wife Christina on May 1, 1811 for $1900.[13] Jacob constructed a beautiful two and one-half story brownstone home which stands today, testament both to the profitable business milling was at the time and the rich agriculture of the region that kept the mill in constant demand. Jacob's estate sold a portion of land that includes the lake and mill to John Hart Kaufman and wife Rachel Griffith Kaufman. In 1845, a farmer, John Hart, sold to John Hart Kaufman the right to the water and access to the millrace between Bennett Run and the lake for the sum of $10.[14] While the documentation has not been found, it is believed that Jacob's estate sold a farmstead to John Hart that included the diversion dam, and the John Hart to John Hart Kaufmann transaction was to secure the water rights to the lake and Kaufman's mill. In the 19th century, deed transfers were not universally recorded as they are today, or a transfer from a half century prior would be recorded contemporaneously with the next transfer, which was being recorded.

The mill passed out of the Kaufman family's hands when John Hart Kaufman sold to Andrew Cline, a farmer from Newberry, in 1852 and moved his family west to Illinois.

Mill Race beneath the former Silver Lake Road Bridge, once powered Lewisberry Mill
(York County History Center)

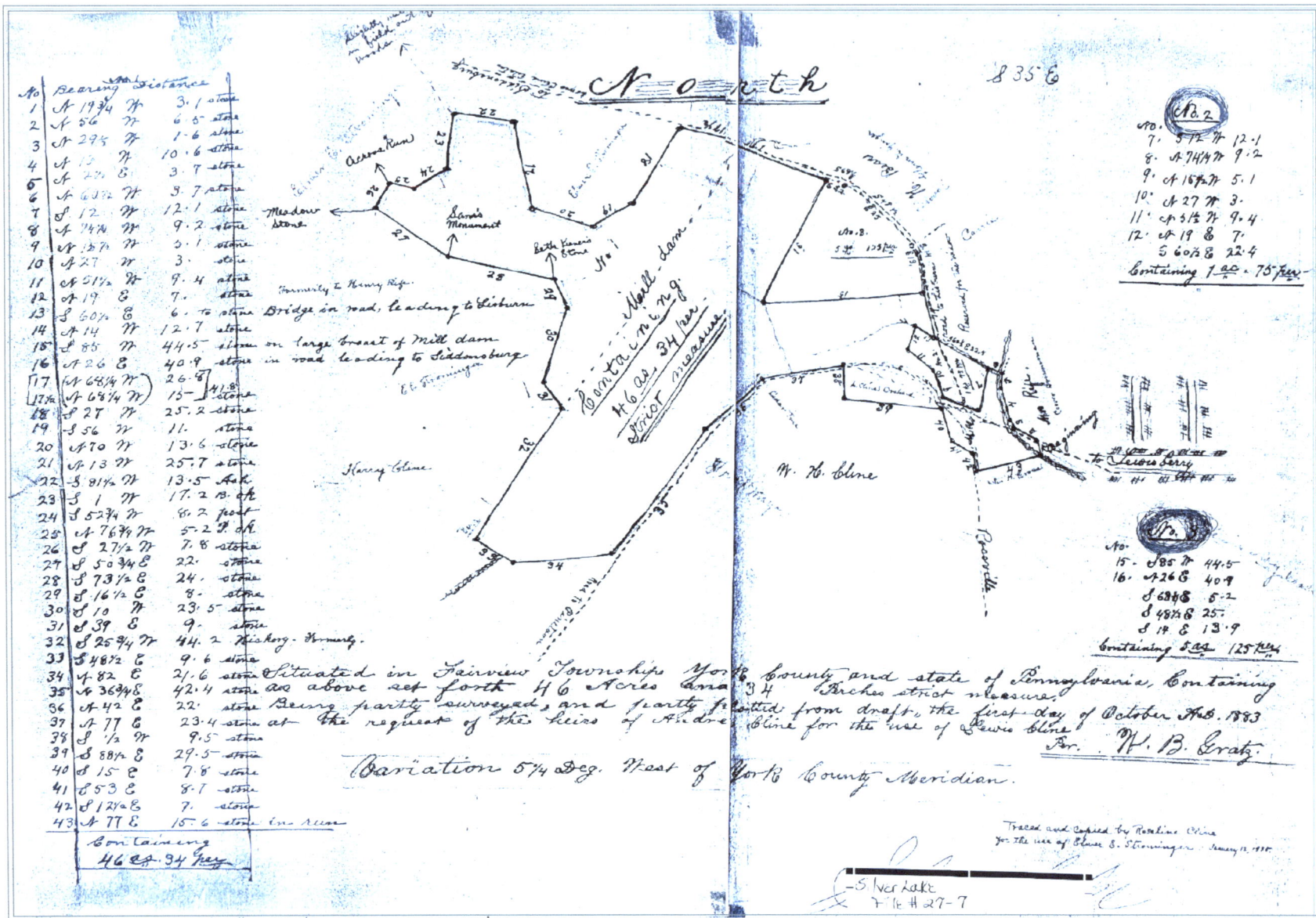

Andrew Cline's mill, mill pond, and surrounding land surveyed for Lewis Cline's use in 1883—replica hand-drawn
and traced by Rosaline Cline at the request of Elmer Ellsworth (E.E.) Strominger in 1935

THE CLINE YEARS

Andrew Cline's purchase: The earthen dam and lush vegetation at Silver Lake's shoreline, thriving in place of cottages, resembling the scenery from W.S. Hammond's youth (Postcard circa 1910)

THE CLINE YEARS

Andrew Cline purchased the mill and all the water rights between the Bennett Run diversion dam and the mill. The transaction was in two deeds, one from John Hart Kaufman of the lake, mill and other buildings for $10,300 ($403,760 in 2024 dollars) dated February 12, 1852.[15] The second deed was from John Hart Kaufman for $10 dated February 16, 1852, yet not recorded until July 28, 1931, that expressly included water rights to include the diversion dam at Bennett Run and the hand dug channel that supplied water to Silver Lake for the mill.[16]

The sale price was indicative of a lucrative operation and both Kaufman and Cline were wise to formally secure these water rights as the original Updegraff track was further subdivided.

Andrew Cline died intestate in 1882. The land was divided between his sons Lewis and Harrison (William Harrison or W.H. Cline) also known as "Harry."[17,18] Lewis Cline bought out his mother and siblings share to the mill, lake, and water rights and Harrison did the same with the farm. Lewis built the lovely Victorian style home, c. 1885, that still stands today. Lewis was the executor of the estate.

John H. Kaufman) Know All Men By These Presents, that John H. Kauffman, the Grantee within
to) named and Rachel his wife, for and in consideration of the sum of Ten
Andrew Clinsfman) Dollars, to them in hand paid by Andrew Cline of Newberry Township in the County of York and State of Pennsylvania at and before the sealing and delivery hereof, the receipt whereof is herebyacknowledged have granted, sold assigned, set over unto the said Andrew Cline his heirs and assigns, all that the within mentioned Water Right, and privileges with all the rights and appurtenances thereunto appertaining;

To have and to hold the said right and privilege with the appurtenances unto the said Andrew Cline his heirs and assigns forever. And the said John H. Kauffman and his heirs

1852 Kaufman Deed to Andrew Cline (Including Water Rights) - Recorded in 1931 (79 years later)

Harrison never married and resided in Jacob and Cristina Kaufman's grand stone mansion[19] with his unmarried sisters, Avis and Carrie, until his passing in 1926. He farmed nearby on land from his late father's estate. After his death, Carrie Cline, his surviving sister, became the sole owner and occupant of the property.[20]

Lewis Cline married Elmira Mordorf in 1871 and the union produced three daughters, Clara, Rosaline, and Edith.[21] Clara married George Coover and together they raised their family in Lemoyne. Rosaline and Edith never married and resided with their parents until Lewis', then Elmira's, deaths. With no heirs to run the mill, Lewis, by 1915-1920, began exploring options as the mill and its technology were becoming obsolete.

The postcard[22] above is believed to be the creation of Rev. J. H. Ricker, a Lewisberry minister who photographed the local area and created postcards.[23] This is the first reference found to the name Silver

Silver Lake Postcard: Reflecting Growing Appreciation Beyond Utility to Recreation

Lake to refer to the Lewisberry mill pond.

Postmarked Lewisberry on September 18, 1913, the postcard was sent from Jake S. to the Honorable Ira "Dan" Weiser of York. It reads, "Dan, This place certainly does appeal to a lover of nature. Look good to you?" This signifies a shift in perspective regarding Silver Lake in the broader community, indicating a growing appreciation beyond its utilitarian function.

With the paving of the "Road to New Cumberland" from Old Trail Road to New Cumberland, Silver Lake became accessible by automobile from Harrisburg and

Majestic Brownstone Residence facing the mill with Silver Lake Road on the left and Siddonsburg
Road and the South Point Schoolhouse to the right (York County History Center)

Premature Plans: No Clear Agreement for
Silver Lake Property Purchase

York and beyond. Any inspiration that Lewis Cline may have had of transitioning Silver Lake from its utilitarian function into a resort would likely have been greatly influenced by the broader Progressive Era in the United States including the Good Roads Movement[24], the City Beautiful movement[25] and President Theodore Roosevelt's era of recreation, conservation, and a deeper appreciation for nature. This transformation held the potential to create new economic opportunities for Lewis Cline and his heirs. Area investors and residents began to recognize Silver Lake for its aesthetic appeal.

Meanwhile, in York, a group of investors formed Silver Lake Incorporated in 1921 to purchase and build a resort and amusement park at Silver Lake, Lewisberry.[26] It does not appear that this group ever reached a satisfactory agreement to purchase the lake and property from Lewis Cline, and trading of Silver Lake Incorporated stock stopped in March 1922.[27]

Lewis Cline died intestate in 1924. His widow and daughters sold the mill, lake, surrounding lands and water rights to William Grant Stonesifer in 1925[28,] reserving a small homestead, the Victorian style home built by Lewis for Elmira and daughters Rosaline and Edith. Lands purchased included a large parcel on the hill east of the lake, frontage along Siddonsburg Road, and limited lakeside frontage along present day Marie, Cardinal and Silver Lake roads.[29] The Cline to Stonesifer deed explicitly defined the water rights specified in earlier deeds to ensure control and consistent water flow to Silver Lake. This deed references various water rights, including those in the Andrew Cline heirs' deeds to Lewis Cline (1884 & 1887).[30]

The following snippet from the Cline to Stonesifer deed[31] does an excellent job describing the historical chain of custody of the property, as well as transferring water rights to Stonesifer and reserving rights to water for the home of the Cline widow and daughters.

16198

Elmira Cline al.
to
William G. Stonesifer

$5.00
Revenue
9-25-25
E.C.

This Indenture, made this twenty fifth day of September in the year of our Lord one thousand nine hundred and twenty five (1925)

Between Elmira Cline (widow) Rosaline Cline, Edith Cline (single women) of Fairview Township, York County and State of Pennsylvania, and Clara Cline Coover and George W. Coover, her husband of Lemoyne, Cumberland County, Penna., grantors and William G. Stonesifer and Mary A. Stonesifer, his wife, of Lemoyne Borough, Cumberland County, State aforesaid, grantees

Witnesseth, that in consideration of five thousand ($5000.00) dollars, in hand paid, the receipt whereof is hereby acknowledged, the said grantors do hereby grant and convey to the said grantees

All the following described two tracts of land situate in Fairview Township, York County Pennsylvania, bounded and limited as follows, viz;

Tract no. 1. Beginning at a stone, thence by land of Carrie Cline North 74¼ degrees West 9.2 perches to a stone; North 15½ degrees West 5.1 perches to a stone; North 27 degrees West

From Deed to Destination:
Elmira Cline et al Deed to
William G. Stonesifer

Water Rights and Boundaries:
Silver Lake property description

perches of land strict measure

Being the same tract of land W. H. Cline, Ann Cline, Carrie Cline, James F. Cline and K. Cline his wife, Eliza Jane Pipher and Stephen C. Pipher her husband, Clarissa Sterrett and Price I. Sterrett her husband, by their deed dated March 10th A. D. 1887, and recorded in Deed Book 9 T, page 348 conveyed to Lewis Cline, who having since died intestate leaving as his survivors and his only legal heirs all over twenty one years old; a widow, Elmira Cline and three daughters Rosaline Cline, Edith Cline and Clara Cline Coover, grantors hereto.

By reference to the afore in part recited deeds, the facts will in full and at large appear

The present grantees shall have the same rights, titles, privileges, and benefits as specified in deeds of January 13th, A. D. 1852 from John H. Kaufman, and Rachel Kaufman his wife to Andrew Cline Said deed about to be recorded

Also deed of February 16th, A. D. 1852 and recorded in Deed Book T. T. T. page 69, from John H. Kaufman and Rachel Kaufman, his wife to Andrew Cline.

Also to have the right and access to the well and full use of the water for household purposes at the dwelling house and land of W. H. Cline, but said water right not to interfere with the water right now held for the dwelling house of the late Lewis Cline, deceased

and the said grantors do hereby covenant and agree to and with the said grantees, that they the grantors, their heirs, executors and administrators shall and will by these presents, warrant and forever defend, the herein above described premises with the hereditaments and appurtenances unto the said grantees, their heirs and assigns, against the said grantors and against every other person lawfully claiming or who shall hereafter claim the same or any part thereof

In witness whereof said grantors have hereunto set their hands and seals the day and year first above written

Sealed and delivered in the presence of
O. W. Barnes
A. B. Bucher

Elmira Cline (seal)
Rosaline Cline (seal)
Edith Cline (seal)
Clara Cline Coover (seal)
George W. Coover (seal)

Shortly after the sale to William G. Stonesifer, Edith Cline penned a narrative about the history of Lewisberry as part of a national Sesqui-Centennial focus and celebration.[32] In her writing, she elaborated on the magnificence of Silver Lake, emphasizing its frequent recognition as an ideal location for a seasonal hotel resort due to its beauty. Edith hinted that this possibility was being considered by a few interested parties. In a subtle disclosure, she pointed out that William G. Stonesifer had recently acquired Silver Lake and the adjoining lands, possessing complete land and water use rights, potentially capable of transforming the area into a resort.

Stonesifer immediately engaged the surveyor Otis H. Barnes from Rossville to plot out approximately 100 lots for small summer cottages.

A short distance west of this house and facing on the Pinetown road is Silver lake, covering an acreage of forty acres. The mill draws its water power from this lake. For generations this was a popular water for fishing, boating and swimming during the summer months and in the winter months the young people from the surrounding country and towns gathered here for skating. On account of the beauty of this lake and a combination of natural attractions this place has often been spoken of as a desirable location for a summer and winter hotel resort. At the present time this matter is underconsideration on the part of a few interested persons.

The mill property, Silver lake and the farm land adjoining has recently been purchased by William G. Stonesifer, of Lemoyne.

Edith Cline's Narrative: Pondering Silver Lake's Attraction as a Potential Seasonal Retreat

THE
STONESIFER
YEARS

William Grant Stonesifer and Mary Alice Keilholtz Wedding Portrait (1890)

(Courtesy of Jillian Stonesifer Teasley)

THE STONESIFER YEARS

William Grant Stonesifer was born on a farm in Adams County in 1866. According to the 1900 and 1910 US Federal Census, he was a farmer and was employed at a sawmill near Biglerville, Adams County (likely along Conewago Creek).[33] He moved his family to Lemoyne, Cumberland County, c. 1919 where he worked in the lumber business.[34]

The intersection of the Cline and Stonesifer families was most likely in Lemoyne. George and Clara Cline Coover raised their family in Lemoyne just blocks away from the Stonesifer household. Several children in the households were close in age and likely attended school together. Newspaper reports in the 1920's and 1930's reported social visits between the two families. In 1928, Guy Stonesifer even constructed a garage on George and Clara Coover's Lemoyne property.

William G. Stonesifer collaborated with Otis H. Barnes to subdivide the Silver Lake lands into small lots. The objective was to create destinations for those seeking a retreat, allowing interaction with nature through activities like fishing and

Before cottages and outhouses, before roads and lots, people converged along the tranquil shores of the lake, seeking solace in nature's embrace (Postcard circa 1910)

boating. The lots on the highly sought after sides of Silver Lake, evidenced by rapid property sales, were intentionally kept small to accommodate as many as possible, while ensuring adequate space by the standards of the era. These parcels were bordered by the lake on one side and by Silver Lake Road and the newly created West Street on the other. Despite additional land being available from the neighboring Strominger farm, the practice of creating small lots persisted on the Cardinal Lane and Marie Avenue sides of the lake.

The creation of small lots on the eastern hill of Silver Lake posed a puzzling scenario. Property owners in this area would acquire small lots that lacked direct lake access, with most not even in sight of the lake. Selling land on the eastern hill proved to be a challenging endeavor, as most of these lots remained unsold for two decades after the initial waterfront lots were sold. Even then, it was necessary to bundle multiple O.H. Barnes' lots together as larger, single parcels, to attract potential buyers. Unfortunately, the original Barnes' subdivision plans are not on record in York County, with only references in various deeds, newspaper articles and subsequent surveys.[35]

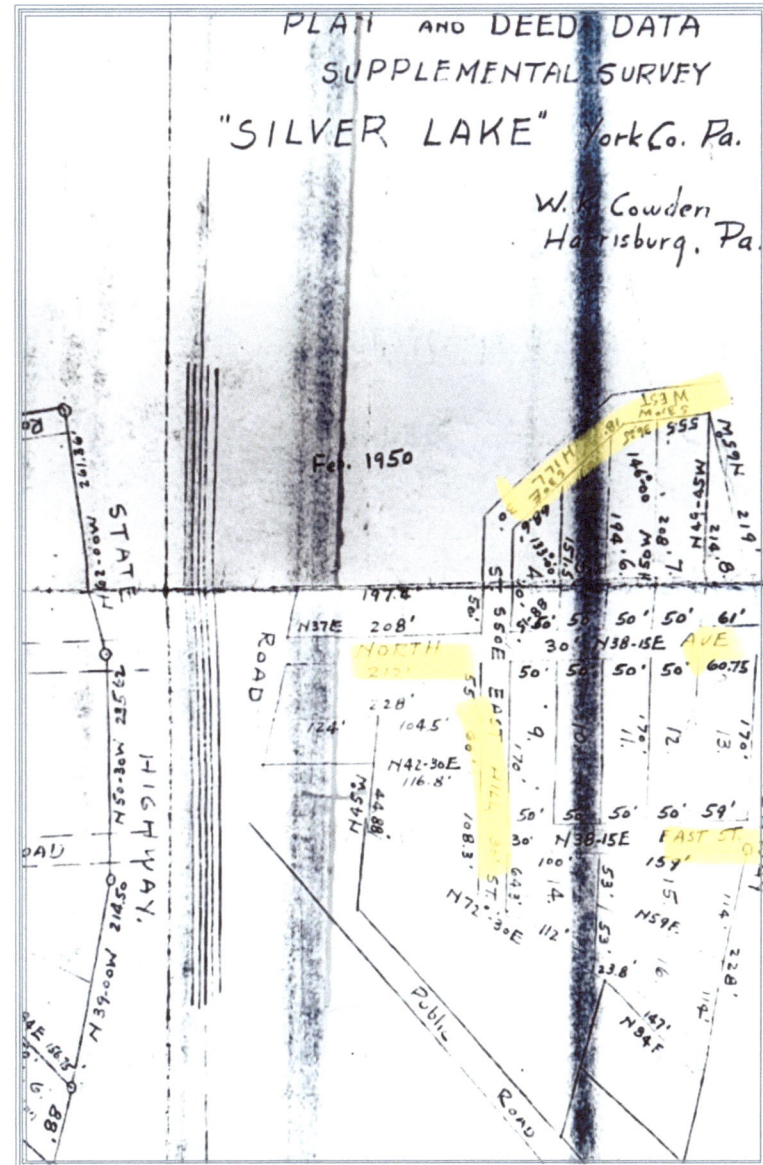

Surveying Silver Lake: W.K. Crowden's Depiction of Small Lots and Access Routes

Shirley Miller Peck Poses by C.H. Desenberg's Cottage, Built
by Guy Stonesifer
(Courtesy of Gary W. Peck)

In 1950, surveyor W.K. Crowden of Harrisburg prepared the "Plan and Deed Data Supplemental Survey of Silver Lake," recreating lot layouts for hillside properties from the Barnes' plan. Due to the lots not directly connecting to established roads, plans were made for gravel roads to grant access. Although several paths were initiated, North Avenue, East Hill Street, West Hill Street, and East Street were left incomplete. Today, some segments of these roads are interconnected as East Street, while others serve as driveways for local residents.

Guy Vernon Stonesifer, aged 26, trained as a carpenter and builder. In the 1930 census he was living with his wife and young son in the first residence in Fairview Township on the macadam road to New Cumberland (described as a bungalow adjacent to the mill, it is likely no longer standing.)[36,37]

Russell Stonesifer, aged 24, and his young wife were living in a rented home on the road to Pinetown (present day Silver Lake Road). Guy spent several years supervising the cutting of roads (paths) and overseeing the building of the retaining walls of present-day West Street and around his father's lot next to the spillway, creating a stone workshop and storage structure, as well as constructing about a dozen cottages on West Street and Silver Lake Road.[38] The stone retaining walls and workshop remain, as well as several cottages, most having been substantially renovated.

The Stonesifer family operated the mill from 1925 to 1933. Guy Stonesifer purchased the mill from his father in 1928. William Stonesifer sold all unimproved lots for $1. William's son, Guy, built many of the early cottages.[39] The family's plans for the financial support necessary to maintain the lake and feeder stream was creative, and worth noting.

Lavina Brown, New Cumberland.
—Mr. and Mrs. Chester Olive, of New Cumberland, and the formers mother, Mrs. Sallier Cline, of Lisburn, visted Miss Carrie Cline.
—Dorsey Stonesifer, of Lemoyne, visted Mr. and Mrs. Guy Stonesifer and Mr. and Mrs. Russel Stonesifer, Silver Lake.
—Guy Stonesifer and Charles

TUESDAY, MAY 21, 19

Gray are building a cottage at Silver Lake for Mr. Hoffman, of Harrisburg. W. G. Stonesifer Lemoyne is also building a cottage at the lake for himself.

Embracing a Timeless Tradition: The Inaugural Cottage
of Six Generations of Family Retreats

Lewisberry

Lewisberry, July 9.—Mr. and Mrs. Guy V. Stonesifer and son, Bobbie, Saturday afternoon attended the funeral services of their aunt, Mrs. Arnold, held at Harrisburg.

The thirteenth cottage at Silver Lake is being erected by C. E. Enseman, of York Haven. Work was begun Saturday morning in charge of Guy V. Stonesifer.

Miss Geraldine Snoke, New Cumberland, is a guest of her grandparents, Mr. and Mrs. Arthur A. Holt.

Mrs. Clara Traver, of near Rossville, is visiting at the home of her brother, W. A. Myers.

Miss Stella Myers, of Jefferson,

Guy Stonesifer's 13th Cottage Brings Resort Vision to Life

The buyers of the $1 lots via deed covenants agreed to collectively pay 50% of the cost of maintaining the dams and streams to the mill owner. Consequently, sales closed in groups so no one individual was left holding that financial commitment alone.

To the right is the record of the initial year of Stonesifer sales: 15 closed in July 1927, with 9 of them closing on the same day, July 16th, 1927.

Newspaper articles indicate that cottages were being constructed at a steady pace.

The beauty of the lake and its environs led to many cottages being given fanciful names! Rustic Nook, Lombardy, Linger Longer, Log Haven, Gibbs Grove (the owners' surname), Green Fairy, and Avalon were some of the cottage names recorded in newspaper articles of the era.

William G. Stonesifer sold approximately 40 lots by 1931, all for $1 plus the obligation to share in the cost of the upkeep of the lake. Perhaps half of the lots had cottages already constructed or under construction.

Table 1: The Initial Year of Stonesifer Lot Sales

Date of Purchase	Property Owner	Location of Property
June 2, 1927	C. M. Senseman	Silver Lake Road
July 2, 1927	Stewart F. Wise	Silver Lake Road
July 2, 1927	Samuel Glassmyer	Silver Lake Road
July 2, 1927	Ivan C. Frey	Silver Lake Road
July 16, 1927	Willis F. Hoffman	West Street
July 16, 1927	Elmer C. Wise	Silver Lake Road
July 16, 1927	John R. Engle	Silver Lake Road
July 16, 1927	Murray J. Landis	West Street
July 16, 1927	Armond H. Rockey	Silver Lake Road
July 16, 1927	W. M. Parthemer	West Street
July 16, 1927	David Hoffman	Silver Lake Road
July 16, 1927	Howard G. Lookingbill	Silver Lake Road
July 16, 1927	Edward Strathmeyer	West Street
July 25, 1927	Ernest T. Masson	West Street
July 26, 1927	Harry E. Swartz	West Street
July 26, 1927	G. H. Hetrick	West Street
December 24, 1927	Claude R. Robins	Cardinal Lane
December 24, 1927	Russell G. Lloyd	Cardinal Lane
December 24, 1927	Frank L. Doughtery	Cardinal Lane

TRAGEDY STRIKES

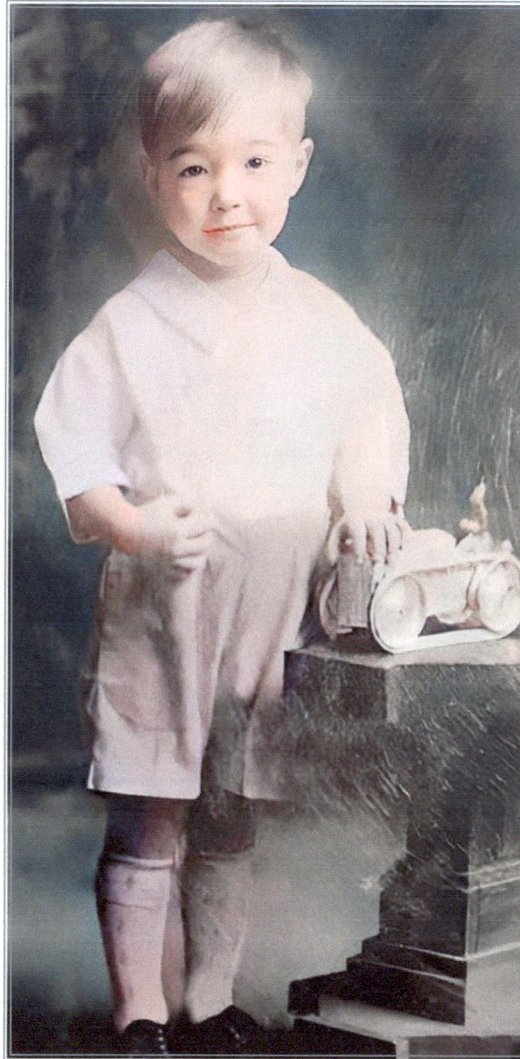

Captured in innocence: Young Bobbie, left fatherless by
the untimely passing of Guy Stonesifer in 1930
(Courtesy of Jillian Stonesifer Teasley)

TRAGEDY STRIKES

Guy Stonesifer, assisted by Charles Gray, was the primary builder erecting the cottages on the lots sold by his father. Unfortunately, Guy Stonesifer died suddenly in the fall of 1930, aged 27, throwing development plans into disarray.

Guy's widow, Mabel, transferred the title to the mill and mill house back to William G. Stonesifer after his death and, with her young son Bobbie, moved away. Russell Stonesifer briefly ran the mill operations, which were slowing down as other transportation options became viable for farm harvest. He also briefly hired a mill operator.

Guy Stonesifer and Mabel: Captured in a Happier Moment
(Courtesy of Jillian Stonesifer Teasley)

The last mill operator located in records was Levi Shaffer, who died in 1933 at age 27 leaving a wife and six sons. The mill was completely decommissioned about that time. In 1939, the Rev. Reinhold Henkelmann obtained two of the original millstones, then abandoned, and incorporated them into his cottage Log Haven's loft railing where they remain today.

William G. Stonesifer's son, Lawrence Clifford "Cliff" Stonesifer, would repurpose the stone mill in the early 1930's as a grocery, gas station and occasional dance hall and, in 1933, leased the property to the Vacumm Oil Company, Inc.[40] Prior to this, he was employed by Troup Brothers' Music, a business owned by E.E. Stominger's brothers-in-law. Cliff eventually purchased the mill property from his father in 1936 and operated the Lewisberry Mills Service Station as the proprietor.[41]

—3—
Shaffer Family Moves

Lewisberry, Feb. 20.—Mrs. Miriam Shaffer and her six sons, Charles, Harold, Levi, Jr., Albert, Stanley and Bobbie removed from the Lewisberry mills house owned by William G. Stonesifer of Lemoyne to a house in Goldsboro. Mrs. Shaffer's husband was killed last May when riding a motorcycle with side car attached on the highway between this place and New Cumberland.

Levi Shaffer: The final mill operator of Lewisberry Mills

Lewisberry Mills Filling Station and Store, L.C. Stonesifer Proprietor
(Courtesy of Robert Griffith)

Preserving History: Original millstones from the Lewisberry Mills in Log Haven
(Authors' Photograph)

William G. Stonesifer relocated to a home in Marsh Run near the present-day New Cumberland Army Depot in 1933. He resided there until his death in 1941.

Russell Stonesifer's rented farmhouse in the vicinity of Silver Lake burned down in 1935 and he and his family moved in with his father William at Marsh Run.[42] Activity slowed in the early years of the depression, and Russell Stonesifer became his father's proxy at Silver Lake. In 1937, William transferred his lakeside cottage to his youngest son Dorsey and appears to have been finished with his Silver Lake aspirations.

36

THE SILVER LAKE IMPROVEMENT COMPANY

Capital Stock Certificate Signed by E.E. Strominger Issued to S. Carroll Miller
(Courtesy of John R. Miller)

THE SILVER LAKE
IMPROVEMENT COMPANY

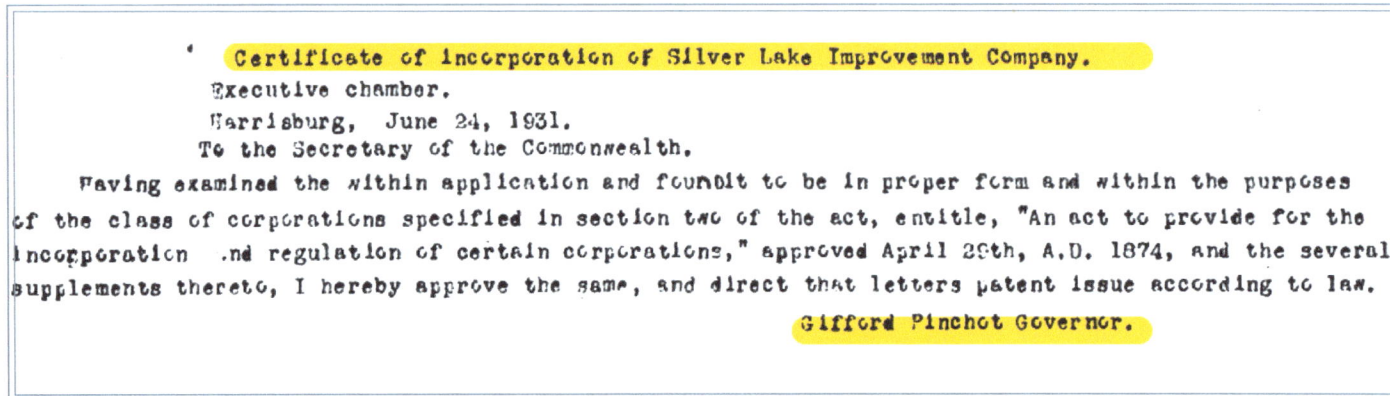

> • Certificate of incorporation of Silver Lake Improvement Company.
> Executive chamber.
> Harrisburg, June 24, 1931.
> To the Secretary of the Commonwealth.
> Having examined the within application and found it to be in proper form and within the purposes of the class of corporations specified in section two of the act, entitle, "An act to provide for the incorporation and regulation of certain corporations," approved April 29th, A.D. 1874, and the several supplements thereto, I hereby approve the same, and direct that letters patent issue according to law.
> Gifford Pinchot Governor.

Governor Gifford Pinchot's Approval Marks Silver Lake Improvement
Company's Official Incorporation

William G. Stonesifer had no family member interested or capable of continuing the development of the summer colony at the lake after the death of his son Guy. Additionally, with the Lewisberry Mills operations winding down, William G. Stonesifer had no financial incentive to continue maintenance of the lake's dams and feeder streams. Silver Lake's future was in peril.

A significant group of the early lot purchasers came together on June 13, 1931 and incorporated Silver Lake Improvement Company[43], capitalized with 100 shares of stock at $50 each, or $5000.

Significant investors were Ivan C. Frey, the proprietor of Spring Garden Brick & Clay Company (Spring Garden, Pennsylvania) and York Colonial Brick Company (York, Pennsylvania), Willis Hoffman, an insurance agent from Spring Garden and one of the first to construct a cottage, Vance H. Loumaster, a colleague in the brick business of Ivan Frey, and also living in Spring Garden, Forry K. Gotwalk, a school teacher in Spring Garden, Doc H. C. Hetrick, a well know Lewisberry physician, Elmer C. Wise, proprietor of the match company in Lewisberry, Ernst Masson, an insurance agent from Harrisburg, E.E.

Strominger and his son-in-law Samuel C. Miller, owners of the large track of land that bordered Stonesifer land on the west side of the lake, and Charles M. Senseman, a tailor and locally known tenor, who purchased the first lot in the William G. Stonesifer subdivision. The formation of the Silver Lake Improvement Company (SLIC) aimed to acquire the Stonesifer family's remaining unsold lots surrounding Silver Lake, along with the lake itself and its feeder streams.

William G. Stonesifer transferred all unsold parcels to SLIC for $1 and the cancellation of his lake maintenance obligations on July 27, 1931, nine months after his son Guy's sudden death. Included in the deed was the transfer of all of the water rights Cline received from Kaufman, Stonesifer from Cline, etc., with Stonesifer reserving the right to use the water from the lake to power the mill.[44]

It is important to note that in the transaction SLIC assumed 50% financial responsibility for the maintenance of the lake, and the lot owners collectively remained responsible for the other 50%.

Although there were still some parcels available on West Street and East Street and Silver Lake Road, SLIC began to develop the lands along Marie Avenue and Cardinal Lane. The Marie Avenue plan of lots is the only remaining documentation of the original subdivision.

Much of the land that Lewis Cline's heirs sold to William G. Stonesifer, who in turn transferred to SLIC, had insufficient land to build cottages along present-day Marie Avenue and Cardinal Lane. The land was essentially the lake's high water point and not much more. The solution was to acquire land from the adjoining Strominger farm.

Purchasers of some SLIC lots acquired land directly from E.E. Strominger, so the deed transfers occurred simultaneously between the two sellers. SLIC, in other instances, purchased segments from Strominger to create salable lots. It is noteworthy that E.E. Strominger, serving as SLIC President as indicated on the stock certificate, along with his son-in-law Samuel Miller, were among the original shareholders of SLIC. This suggests a deliberate plan of cooperation from the inception of SLIC.

In the O.H. Barnes' Marie Avenue subdivision, the notation at the bottom left states it's for the south side of Silver Lake, but it actually shows the north side. Additionally, it appears that this document was layered on top of another from O.H. Barnes' Silver Lake Plan of Lots when photographed for the York County Recorder of Deeds. The York County Government archive holds solely the Marie Avenue Plan of Lots; no other plans have been located by the staff.

The remainder of the 1930's saw the sale of lots primarily on Marie Avenue and Cardinal Lane, until, by the time World War II broke out, there were only a handful of remaining lots from the original plan of lots on the east side of the lake, up the hill, none of which had water frontage. Henry A. Torchia and other Torchia family members, a first-generation Italian immigrant family from Harrisburg, purchased most of the remaining SLIC lots in 1946, and L.C. "Cliff" Stonesifer repurchased the last lots previously sold to SLIC by his father.[45] 1946 marked the end of the Silver Lake Improvement Company's development activities.[46]

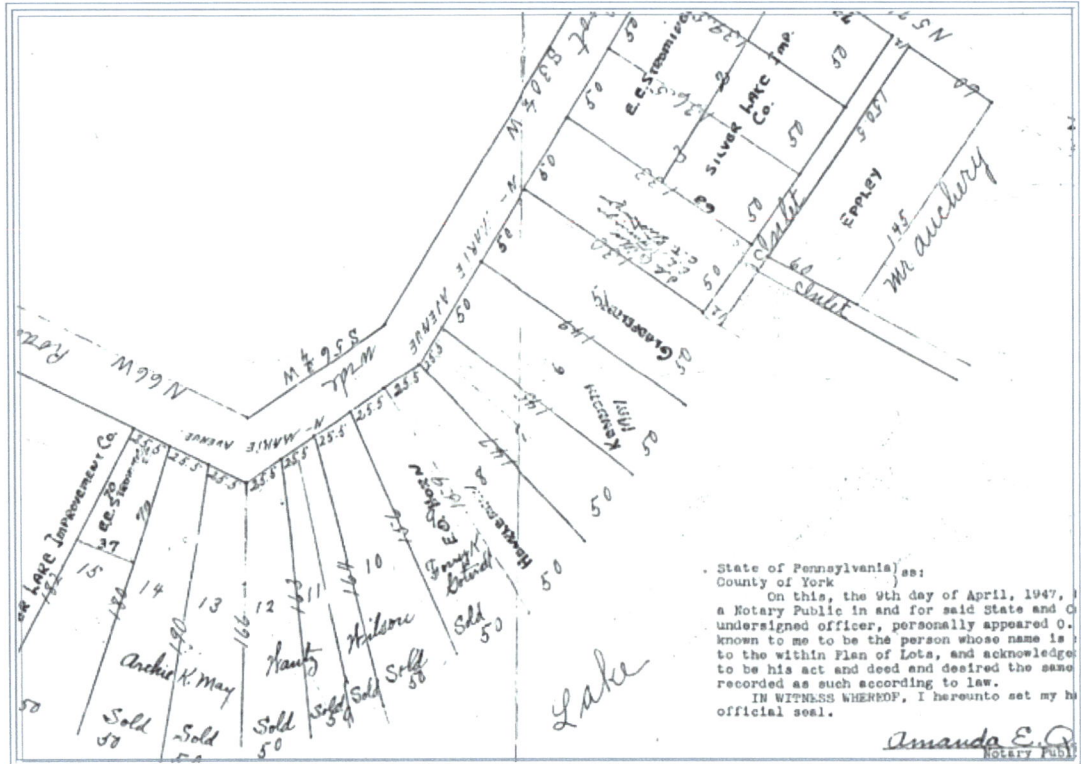

Recorded subdivision of the land along Marie Avenue, including the owners of sold lots

Mission Complete: Silver Lake Improvement
Company Closes Its Doors

DISSOLUTION NOTICE
Notice is hereby given that Silver Lake Improvement Company, a business corporation organized and existing under the laws of the Commonwealth of Pennsylvania, with its registered office in Lewisberry, Pennsylvania, has elected to dissolve voluntarily and to wind up its affairs; and that on the 12th day of March, 1948, has filed with the Department of State, Harrisburg, Pennsylvania, a certificate of election to dissolve, and that the Board of Directors of said corporation is winding up and settling the affairs of said corporation for the purposes of dissolution.
Silver Lake Improvement Company.
T. Frederick Feldmann,
   Solicitor.   14-27j

THE SILVER LAKE COMMUNITY ASSOCIATION

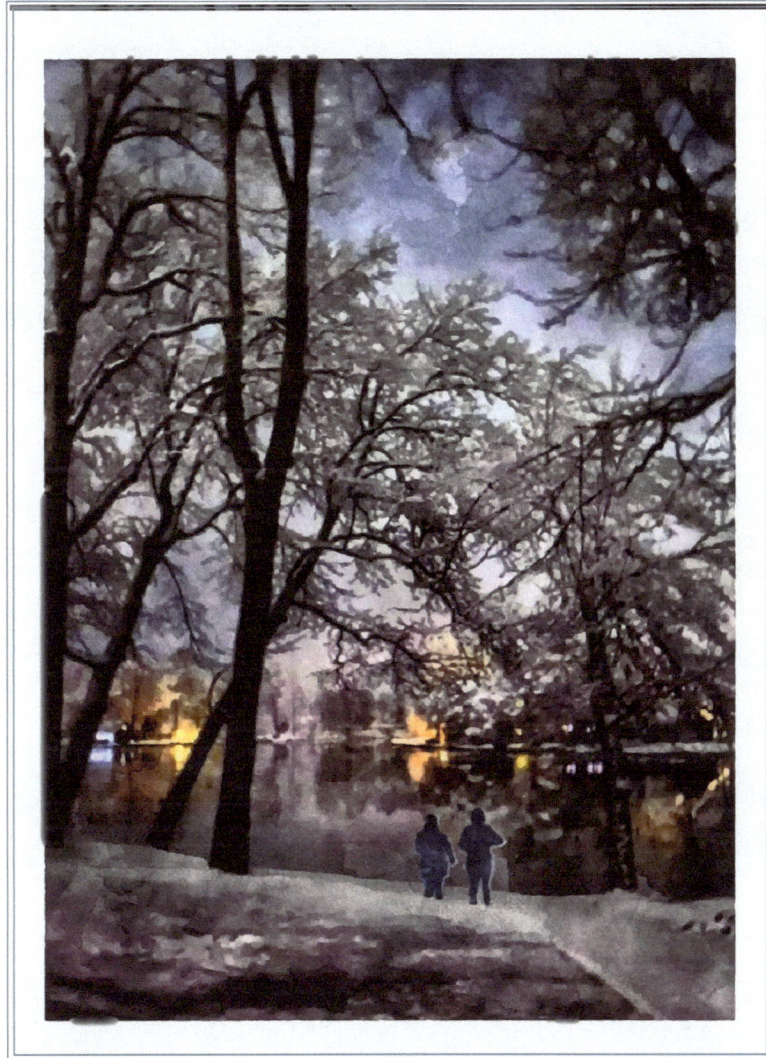

Beneath snow-draped branches, observing association
members' bonfires aglow in the distance across Silver Lake
(Courtesy of B. Himes)

THE SILVER LAKE COMMUNITY ASSOCIATION

The Silver Lake Improvement Company, foreseeing the sale of the remaining lots, initiated the closure of its operations and sought to transfer the lake, feeder streams, and dams from its responsibility. In January 1946, upon the Commonwealth of Pennsylvania's recognition of its Articles of Incorporation, the Silver Lake Community Association (SLCA) became a Pennsylvania nonprofit corporation.[47]

Commonwealth of Pennsylvania   :   ARTICLES OF INCORPORATION OF SILVER LAKE COM-

                        To   :   MUNITY ASSOCIATION

Silver Lake Community Association: TO THE HONORABLE, THE JUDGES OF THE COURT OF

                                                COMMON PLEAS OF YORK COUNTY, PENNSYLVANIA:

The undersigned subscribers respectfully represent:

That they are citizens of the Commonwealth of Pennsylvania and have associated themselves together for the purpose of acquiring ownership of Silver Like and adjoining lands situate in Fairview Township, York County, Pennsylvania, together with water rights therein and promoting the general welfare of the summer colony known as Silver Lake, and being desirous of becoming incorporated, agreebly to the provisions of the Non-Profit Corporation Law of the Commonwealth of Pennsylvania, approved the 5th day of May A. D. 1933, and the supplements thereto and the

Formally Recognized: Silver Lake Community Association by the Commonwealth of Pennsylvania

The Silver Lake Community Association was created to acquire ownership of Silver Lake and promote the well-being of the summer colony known as Silver Lake. The term "summer colony," notably a legal term, refers to places primarily intended for seasonal vacation or recreational stays by families or adults for hire.[48] The individuals founding this association aimed to safeguard their investments in lots and cottages, whether for personal use or as rental properties, to avoid any impact from potential lake disrepair. The Articles of Incorporation further elaborate by delineating the following purposes to:

Protect the water rights of the body of water known as Silver Lake, in Fairview Township, York County, Pennsylvania; maintain the feeder streams to Silver Lake in proper condition to allow the free flow of water to the lake, and to maintain the present charter rights to these streams; fostering cooperative effort of all property owners to preserve the best possible conditions in the summer colony known as Silver Lake, pertaining to sanitary, social, and economic affairs and the general welfare of the community without profit to the corporation; and acquiring ownership of Silver Lake and adjoining lands situate in Fairview Township, York County, Pennsylvania together with water rights therein.

A Turning Point: Ownership of Silver Lake Transferred to SLCA in 1948

All the land located between their present retaining walls or natural lake front boundaries as they are now located and built along the share of Silver Lake and the front lines of their respective properties as the same may be recited in the respective deeds whereby they acquired title to their said properties.

The land herein released and quit-claimed being a part of the same premises which the Silver Lake Improvement Company, a Pennsylvania corporation, by its deed dated January 30, 1948, granted and conveyed unto the Silver Lake Community Association, a Pennsylvania corporation.

Restoring Rights: SLCA returns land using Quit Claim Deed

On February 6, 1948, ownership of the lake, dams, and streams was transferred to the Silver Lake Community Association. This occurred two years after the SLCA was incorporated. Five weeks later, on March 12, 1948, the Silver Lake Improvement Company was dissolved.[49]

To facilitate the sale, all lakefront property owners allowed a survey of their land, extending a few feet from the water's edge, and incorporated it into the lake property transfer deed. The term 'on the water's edge' was deemed too vague for precise property transfers, given its variability with changing water levels. To prevent permanent land relinquishment, the newly formed SLCA acted immediately to return the land. On February 13, 1948, the SLCA recorded a Quit Claim Deed for all lakefront property owners, renouncing any claim and surrendering roughly 3 feet of land between the owners' lakeside property line and the lakeshore or retaining walls to those owning lakeside properties.[50]

For a small group of owners of approximately 50 summer cottages, they were incredibly organized, with committees that residents vied to participate in. There was the Membership Committee, Nomination Committee, Sanitary Committee, Decoration Committee, Legal Committee, Dams and Streams Committee, even the Police Committee. Residents embraced a new era of shared responsibility and stewardship over the serenity and beauty that was Silver Lake.

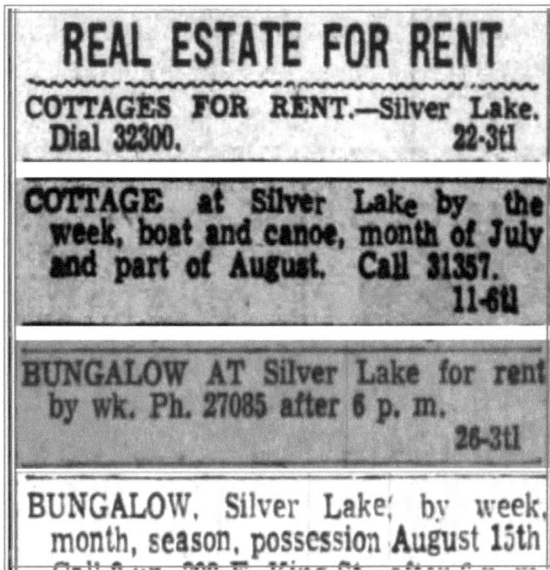

REAL ESTATE FOR RENT

COTTAGES FOR RENT.—Silver Lake.
Dial 32300.   22-3tl

COTTAGE at Silver Lake by the
week, boat and canoe, month of July
and part of August. Call 31357.
                               11-6tl

BUNGALOW AT Silver Lake for rent
by wk. Ph. 27085 after 6 p. m.
                               26-3tl

BUNGALOW, Silver Lake, by week,
month, season, possession August 15th

Silver Lake Cottage Rentals by Investor-Owners

Regarding membership, joining the SLCA, even for residents near the lake, wasn't automatic. Prospective members were required to submit a membership application, which needed endorsement by a majority of the Membership Committee before being recommended to the Board of Directors. Final approval was granted via a majority vote by the Board of Directors. Membership revocation was possible by the Board of Directors

if dues remained unpaid, 30 days after the member received written notification.

Silver Lake was very much a summer colony at this time. [51] While speaking to members of the Torchia family, who purchased the last lots from Silver Lake Improvement Company and lived on "Torchia Hill" as the area up behind present day West Street was referred to mid-20th century, their homes had indoor plumbing and septic fields. The summer cottages along the water still had outdoor pumps and out houses. Families in off-lake properties had very little interaction with the seasonal, summer-only, families in the lakeside cottages.

H. Andrew "Andy" Torchia Jr. observed that it wasn't just a divide of summer only vs. year-round residents, but also a physical divide as access to other sides of the lake from their homes on the

hill required cutting through summer cottages' property and crossing the dam or spillway, both activities forbidden by their parents.

For the year-round residents, winter was when the lake really shined! Ice skating, bonfires, cook outs abounded when the lake was frozen. Local lore has it that Sonja Henie, the famous Olympic figure skater, practiced on Silver Lake in January 1937 when she was in the area to perform special intermission programs during Hershey Bears professional hockey games.

A decade later, Silver Lake faced a threat to its very existence. [52] One will recall that when the mill was constructed and the lake created by the first settlers, a diversion dam and hand dug diversion channel was constructed from Bennett Run to the lake site to provide a continuous source of water to power the mill. Without this stream, or race as it is sometimes referred to as, there is no lake.

The Kaufman family, in the 1850's, had the foresight to secure the legal rights to this diversion dam and resulting stream when the land was being subdivided amongst heirs. Such rights were passed on upon sale to the Clines, and later the Stonesifers, SLIC, and SLCA.

In 1956 -1957, the owners of the property upon which the diversion dam resides, took steps to remove the dam and redirect water flow from the mill stream. The SLCA took action legally, and once again secured the rights to the dam and stream.[52]

It is unclear with remaining records whether there was a financial settlement or how much it might have been. What is known is that the SLCA secured rights to access the dam on the bank facing the town of Lewisberry for maintenance of the diversion dam and the stream bed to maintain steady water flow to the lake.

DAMAGE SUIT FILED

Dispute Over Ownership of Mill
Race Near Silver Lake to
Be Aired in Court

An action in equity was filed in Common Pleas Court yesterday by the Silver Lake Community Association of Lewisberry R. D. 1 against Mr. and Mrs. Hugh A. Taylor, 2435 Camby street, Harrisburg, and involving a dispute over ownership of a mill race near Silver Lake.

The association contends in its complaint that it has title to Bennett's run and mill race which provides water for the lake. The run and mill race are located on the land of the Taylors.

The county association, which includes members who own property adjacent to the lake, contend the Taylors have removed stones from the dam, diverting water from the mill race; have pulled tree stumps and excavated land around the dam; have removed dirt from above the dam and deposited automobiles, trash stones and other debris in the water course to divert water away from the mill race.

The court was asked to enjoin the defendants from continuing to alter the property, to reimburse the plaintiffs for $150 spent on repairs and award the Silver Lake group $25,000 punitive damages.

The association claims title and water rights in Bennett's run and mill race by virtue of deeds dating back to 1845. The suit was filed by Attorneys Russell F Griest and Richard P Noll on behalf of the association, which claims the defendants' action has caused the lake's water level to drop and deprived them of the enjoyment of fishing, boating and swimming on the lake.

PUBLIC HEALTH CONCERNS AND DEVELOPMENT TRANSFORM SILVER LAKE

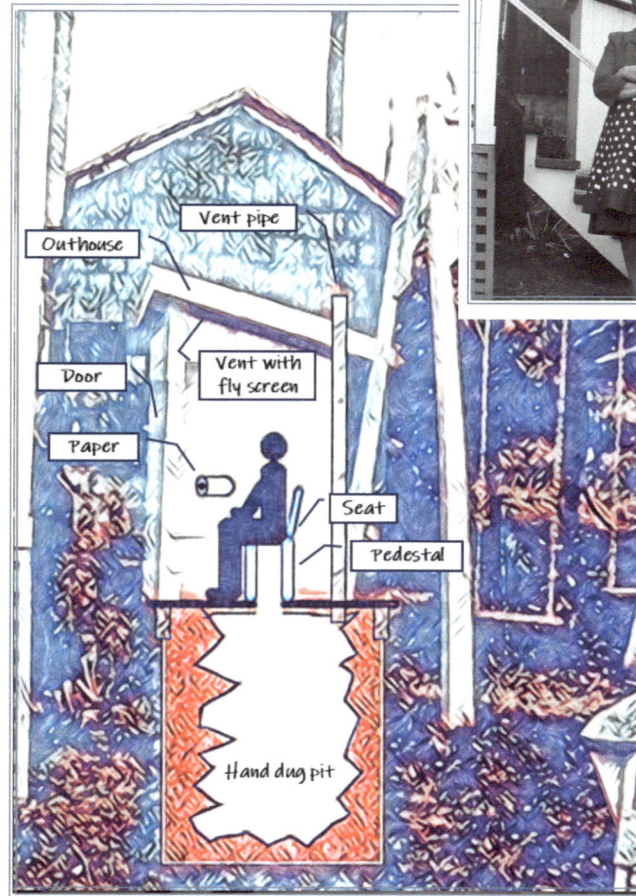

A cutaway cross section sketch revealing the inner workings of an outhouse once used at Silver Lake cottage until 1989. (Authors' illustration)

PUBLIC HEALTH CONCERNS AND DEVELOPMENT TRANSFORM SILVER LAKE

Residents of Lewisberry Borough began investigating solutions to their longstanding sewer and water issues, especially in the borough and the Silver Lake area, in the 1960's.[53] Most of the lakeside cottages still had outhouses, and the lots were not large enough to implement septic fields needed for sanitary plumbing. A feasibility study regarding public sewers was commissioned in 1966 by Lewisberry Borough. Fairview Township, which borders the borough and where Silver Lake resides, declined to participate. In 1971, as sanitation concerns heightened, the borough commissioned an updated study with special attention to the area around Silver Lake and ceded authority to enforce health laws from the borough managers to the Commonwealth of Pennsylvania. A significant concern of the borough was that sewage from Silver Lake was entering Bennett Run as it ran along the border of Lewisberry Borough.

A 1977 study by the Northern York County Regional Joint Sewage Authority found that seven percent of Fairview County residences, many clustered around Silver Lake, still used privies, a significant source of contamination of local waterways.[54]

In 1985 the Lewisberry Area Joint Authority was formed to provide sewage services to the borough of Lewisberry.[55] A sanitary sewer system was constructed in 1986–1988 and all properties with private septic or privies were required to connect to the public sewer by the end of 1989.

The introduction of sanitary sewers ushered in a dramatic change to the nature of the Silver Lake community. It's status as a "summer" resort quickly ended. Over a period of less than a decade, a majority of the cottages had been remodeled, often enlarged, to include indoor plumbing for kitchens and baths, and became year-round dwellings. The lake was no longer the primary focus of the community as residents commuted to Mechanicsburg, Harrisburg, York, and the like for work, raised their families, and attended sporting and other community events away from the lake.

Silt buildup is always an issue with man-made lakes, and the transformation of nearby farmland to housing developments exacerbated the issue for Silver Lake. Storm water run-off ran faster, and the lake rose more quickly after weather events. The silt was piling up.

In the early 1990's, several permanent residents worked together, with financial support from other lake property owners, to create a silt retention pond on the Bennet Run mill race ahead of its entrance to the lake. Heavy equipment was brought in, and tons of silt was dredged from the lake. It was a heroic effort, resulting in a disappointing mere 4-6" improvement in the lake depth. Lacking leadership and a funding source, the effort was abandoned.

LOOKING FORWARD

Protected Species: Bald Eagle
(Courtesy of Ken Boyer)

LOOKING FORWARD

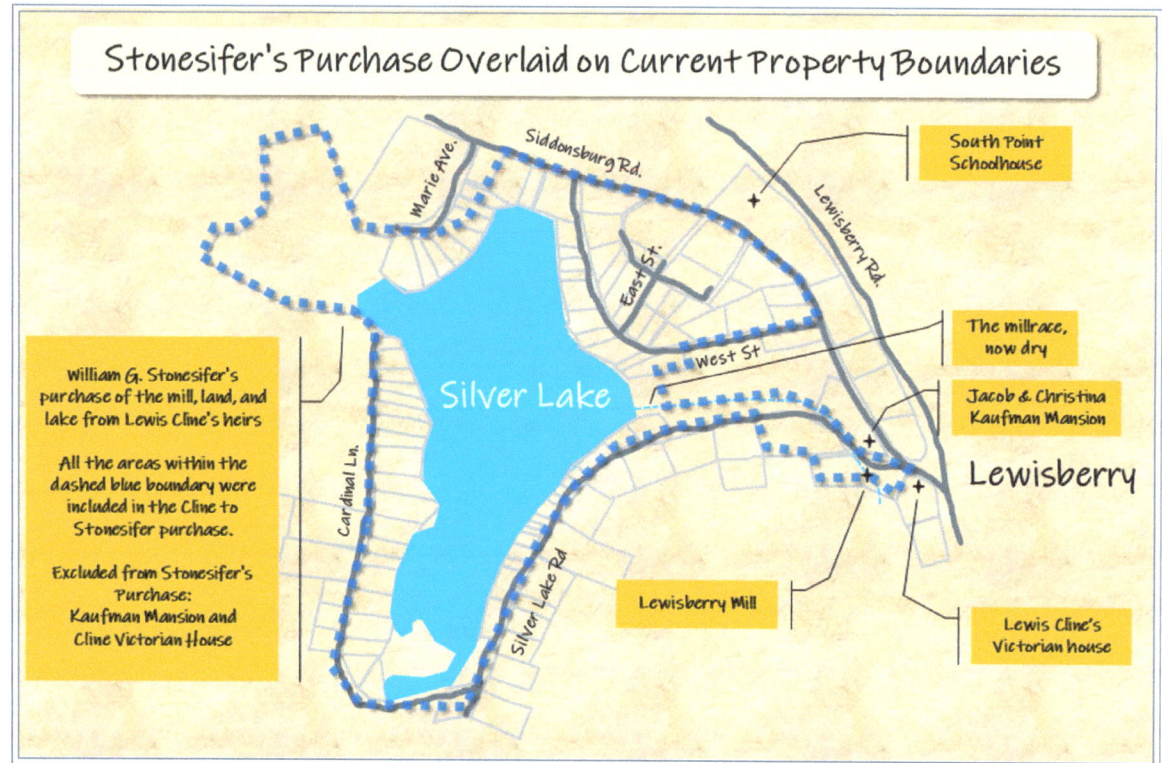

Stonesifer's Purchase Overlaid on Current Property Boundaries

William G. Stonesifer's acquisition of Lewis Cline's mill, lake, and the land areas defined by the dotted blue line, as overlaid upon today's property boundaries (Authors' illustration)

William G. Stonesifer's purchase of the mill, land, and lake from Lewis Cline's heirs

All the areas within the dashed blue boundary were included in the Cline to Stonesifer purchase.

Excluded from Stonesifer's Purchase: Kaufman Mansion and Cline Victorian House

South Point Schoolhouse

The millrace, now dry

Jacob & Christina Kaufman Mansion

Lewisberry

Lewisberry Mill

Lewis Cline's Victorian house

Silver Lake

Siddonsburg Rd.

Marie Ave.

East St.

Lewisberry Rd.

West St.

Cardinal Ln.

Silver Lake Rd.

Silver Lake fell under the purview of the Pennsylvania Department of Environmental Protection (PA DEP), and in 2013 was reclassified as a Class 2 High Hazard dam. Engineering standards have evolved over time, and Silver Lake's earthen dam constructed in the 18th century did not meet 21st century standards. Additionally, residential homes were constructed over time in the area below the dam, thus creating a risk to life and property in the event of a dam failure.

The SLCA and residents have been working steadily since that time to engineer an acceptable and financially reasonable modification to the dam structure to meet current safety standards and to preserve this 250-year-old lake and community for the future.

THE CURIOUS CASE OF SILVER LAKE INCORPORATED

THIS WILL ANSWER THAT QUESTION—Who has so far invested in

SILVER LAKE

Incorporated

"The Ideal Summer Resort?"

LeGrand Dutcher, President   C. L. McKenzie, General Manager

Haines, the Shoe Wizard	J. F. Zeigler	Mrs. C. L. McKenzie
J. L. Getz, Whistle Bottling Co.	C. W. Mann	W. E. Brenneman
Wm. Harlacker, confectionery	Mrs. C. W. Mann	C. H. Wilson
Zeigler Candy Co.	V. A. Stein	Robert Smith
H. N. Forrey, Sanitary Milk Co.	Geo. Small	Constance Smith
Diehl Candy Co.	H. E. Jacobs	Alice Craven
J. H. Desenberg	E. J. Best, restaurant	R. L. Binder
Mrs. J. Weigand	A. S. Kerr	L. S. Osgood
F. H. Welsh	C. Livingston	J. L. Brock
J. F. Wood	J. R. Tracey	W. C. Shellenberger
H. A. Wisotske	Mrs. Wm. Trullinger	P. W. Aughenbaugh
G. H. Hummel, Maple Press	T. Holler	T. B. Leidig
B. Feldman	M. S. Smith	Mrs. S. B. Gray
C. C. Neff	Geo. Watson	H. J. Maul
H. Kottmeier	Mrs. Geo. Watson	J. F. Magee
G. K. Shearer, druggist	M. H. Fink	R. L. Marquart
E. W. Munns	L. Butler	J. I. Gramling
J. K. Bury	P. R. Schweitzer	C. H. Kline
J. W. Robison	E. Lindblom	J. W. Robinson
G. N. Ottmyer	C. A. Hoffman	H. Coburn
M. H. Harris	Mrs. A. L. McKenzie	

"What is good for them is good for you"

A postal addressed Silver Lake, P. O. Box 373, York, Pa., will bring you SILVER LAKE NEWS every week, FREE. You will find it very interesting reading matter..

Silver Lake: The Ideal Summer Resort

THE CURIOUS CASE OF SILVER LAKE INCORPORATED

Silver Lake Lewisberry to be Made into Amusement Park

SILVER LAKE, LEWISBERRY, TO BE MADE INTO AMUSEMENT PARK

...little lake at Lewis-... known as Silver ...graphical charts, ...ers has been the ... line family, will ...over by a company ...zed to establish an ...there. The pic-...together with its ...between York and ...about the same dis-...isle and Mechanics-... the fact that both the Susquehanna trail and the state road will make it accessible to motorists, is expected to make the park a success.

The fact that such a beautiful body of water is located so near to York will be a revelation to many people, for, although within several hundred feet of the main road, the lake is hidden from view by a small hill. The lake abounds with fish and is fed by little streams of pure spring water, none of which comes in contact with any organic matter.

Facilities for bathing, boating and fishing will be provided. The average depth of the lake is six feet and its greatest depth 20 feet. It is about two miles in circumference. The part to be used for swimming, about three acres, has a sandy bottom and will be improved.

Promoters hope to make Silver Lake the greatest automobile resort in the state and the first of a chain of parks devoted entirely to autoists. It is understood that a bus line from York and Harrisburg will be ... ganized and persons not owning ... tomobiles will be given an op... tunity to secure membership. ... McKenzie, local agent for the U... News company, will be the man... of the new park. Option on ... than 70 acres of ground now o... by H. Cline, W. H. Cline and C... Cline have been signed and the ... tire lake, including the mill prop... will be taken over by the comp... It is expected that the park wi... opened to members and friends ...

During the late 19th and early 20th centuries, amusement parks witnessed a remarkable surge in popularity, firmly establishing themselves as a widely embraced source of entertainment. The advent of transportation advancements, particularly railroads and automobiles, facilitated travel and encouraged people to explore areas beyond the confines of urban life. As wages increased, coupled with the implementation of the five-day work week (standardized by Henry Ford in 1926), individuals found themselves with the time, disposable income, and opportunities to explore the diverse attractions offered by these parks. These attractions included roller coasters, Ferris wheels, carousels, sideshows, and a range of live entertainment options. Furthermore, to seek respite from the summertime heat in the cities, developers often located the parks near tranquil lake and river settings. These settings invited visitors to commune with nature, organize picnics, and partake in water-based activities like swimming, fishing, and boating. This marked the golden age of amusement parks. In central Pennsylvania, numerous parks emerged, including Hershey Park in Hershey, Rocky Springs Park in Lancaster, and the Williams Grove Amusement Park, in Williams Grove.

It was during this time of widespread popularity of amusement parks, and their recognition as prosperous ventures, that

Lake at Lewisberry – not Lewistown – to be made into a resort

LeGrand Dutcher and C.L. McKenzie arrived in Lewisberry with the intention of exploring Silver Lake as a potential location for an amusement park.

In a news article published in 1921, the concept of transforming Silver Lake into an amusement park was presented to the public.[56] Although the article's tone was more promotional than news, it proposed that a Silver Lake amusement park could become the premier automobile resort in the state. The promoters envisioned it as the flagship park in a series of attractions specifically designed to cater to motorists.

The article highlighted the crucial factors for a successful amusement park: proximity to a scenic water body like Silver Lake, closeness to population centers such as York and Harrisburg, and easy accessibility via modern roads for car travelers. It mentions that Silver Lake Incorporated secured over 70 acres of land from H. Cline, W. H. Cline, and Carrie Cline, with C.L. McKenzie, a Union News agent, appointed as the manager.

In January 1922 - six weeks after the introductory news story about the Silver Lake amusement park - an advertisement sought individuals who "can tell the truth about the most wonderful summer resort" and aimed to recruit them as salespersons for Silver Lake Incorporated.[57]

In early February 1922, right after the sales staff ad, another one surfaced in the Harrisburg Telegraph and York Dispatch. It asked, "Who's invested in Silver Lake Incorporated, the ideal summer resort?[58] Listing 60+ investor names, it implied vetting and financial backing, fostering trust for potential investors. Readers met LeGrand Dutcher, President of Silver Lake Incorporated, for the first time. The ad closed by noting that readers could receive the Silver Lake News weekly by requesting it from Silver Lake Incorporated, aiding in potential investor collection. However, subscribers eventually received just two newsletters.

On February 22, 1922, Silver Lake Incorporated published their final ad titled, "Please Don't Be Impatient," highlighting numerous stock sales.[59] The advertisement stated that their stock certificates had run out and that temporary yellow receipts would serve as substitutes until regular forms could be printed.

Join Our Team: Seeking Honest Sales Professionals for Silver Lake Incorporated

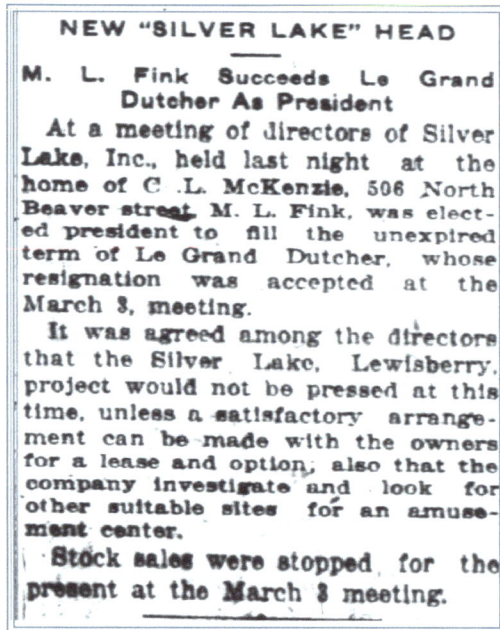

NEW "SILVER LAKE" HEAD

M. L. Fink Succeeds Le Grand Dutcher As President

At a meeting of directors of Silver Lake, Inc., held last night at the home of C .L. McKenzie, 506 North Beaver street, M. L. Fink, was elected president to fill the unexpired term of Le Grand Dutcher, whose resignation was accepted at the March 3, meeting.

It was agreed among the directors that the Silver Lake, Lewisberry, project would not be pressed at this time, unless a satisfactory arrangement can be made with the owners for a lease and option; also that the company investigate and look for other suitable sites for an amusement center.

Stock sales were stopped for the present at the March 3 meeting.

This Article Marks the Dissolution of Silver Lake Incorporated Amusement Park

Eleven days later, on March 3, 1922, a directors' meeting was held at the residence of C.L. McKenzie, according to an April 6, 1922 article in The York Dispatch.[60] During the meeting, LeGrand Dutcher resigned, and M.L. Fink was elected as the new president to complete Dutcher's unexpired term. The directors also made the decision not to proceed with the Silver Lake project unless they could secure a lease and an option from the lake's owners. As a result of this meeting, stock sales were halted, effectively marking the end of Silver Lake Incorporated.

What could have motivated Dutcher and McKenzie to take this path? Initially, the steady demand for amusement parks indicated a promising opportunity. The straightforward nature of running an amusement park business had its own appeal. The stock advertisements in the York Daily Record for other amusement parks demonstrated an excellent route for fundraising. [61]

Furthermore, Mr. McKenzie's confidence may have been bolstered as he witnessed the successful 1922 construction of the York City Farquhar Park community swimming pool[62] mere yards from his home.[63] Additionally, the establishment and subsequent operation of the White Rose Amusement Park in 1926[64],

also located within 100 yards of his York residence, could have made the prospect of success appear quite attainable. The promise of prosperity could have been a compelling factor.

However, reality was quite different. In a span of only 76 days, the Silver Lake Incorporated business venture emerged, underwent a short but intense period of fundraising through stock sales, and eventually faced its dissolution. Despite its ambitious nature, this endeavor never gained traction primarily due to its failure to secure the rights from Lewis Cline to use the lake and the surrounding acreage. This foundational issue doomed the venture from the very beginning.

Amusement park once thrilled city

The city swimming pool, built in 1923, is the remaining part of the White Rose Amusement Park, which also featured carousel, roller coaster, bandstand and miniature golf course.

Mr. and Mrs. Fred Brothell started the park in mid-1923. It was the city's key attraction. The park was eventually sold to Sam McCall and Charles Helm, who kept it running early in the 1930s, according to a booklet published by Northwest Civic Association (Charles Vaught.

In the 1930s, the White Rose Amusement Park included a bandstand, carousel, roller coaster and other entertainment. All that remains

White Rose Amusement Park York, PA

Farquhar Park Pool, York Pennsylvania – Opened July 8, 1922

"RENDEZVOUS"
—ATLANTIC CITY'S NEW PARK

People Go to Atlantic City to Spend Money

THE quarter of a million visitors who, each summer day, make the famous Boardwalk and the beach a spectacular maze of movement and color, are bent on recreation and pleasure. And they have come with money to spend. In the carnival spirit they come, they spend, they go. But Atlantic City goes on forever—it is a national institution.

And there is not a single amusement park in Atlantic City! Imagine the popularity of a high-grade amusement park located right on the busiest section of the Boardwalk. Think of the thousands who will pack it to capacity every day of June, July, August and September. Figure for yourself the profits that will be made by the company operating this Park.

Join This Profitable Business—The Boardwalk Park Company of Atlantic City will build such a park this summer. It will have 150 feet frontage on the Boardwalk, in the heart of the fashionable hotel district, between the Ambassador, and the Marlborough-Blenheim and Traymore. The Pennsylvania, the Reading, and the Electric Railroads unload their crowds of excursionists at the very door of the Park. The location could not be better.

This Company is offering you an opportunity to participate in its profits. It is capitalized for 100,000 shares of common stock, par value $25.00 per share. There is no preferred stock. You can buy this stock now for $15.00 per share.

Safe Investment—High Returns—Conservative estimates place the income of the Company for a

season at better than $1,500,000. This is based on an attendance of no more than 10% of the 250,000 daily visitors, and on the supposition that each will spend only 50 cents. Profits from popular amusements are high under ordinary circumstances. Experts believe that in the case of this Park they *cannot* amount to less than $500,000 a year. This is enough to pay $5.00 per share on the stock. —or 33⅓% on your investment.

Do Not Delay—This is an unusual proposition. It is sound; it is profitable. The officers of the Company, and Board of Directors, prominent business men and amusement park experts, are a guarantee of the management and security of the undertaking. The need for this park at Atlantic City and the splendid location on which it will be built guarantee its success.

Executive Officers

S. BERNARD NOVEMBER, President · ELLWOOD SALSBURY, Vice President and General Manager
HARRY M. CAMPBELL, Secretary and Treasurer

Board of Directors

C. E. ADAMS
Real Estate and Insurance
C. J. Adams Co., Atlantic City, N.J.

ARTHUR ARMSTRONG
Real Estate
Philadelphia and Atlantic City

PAUL CLELAND,
Director
U.S. Copper Products Corporation
West Virginia Metal Products Corp.
The Parish Paul Company
The Long Body Company

HARRY M. CAMPBELL
Baltimore

WM. H. DREWYERS
Manufacturer of Chemicals
Philadelphia and Atlantic City

S. BERNARD SALSBURY
Director, Minneapolis and St. Louis
Railroad

ELLWOOD SALSBURY
Ingersoll Construction Co., Pittsburg

AMBASSADOR · RITZ CARLTON · SHELBURNE · MARLBOROUGH BLENHEIM · TRAYMORE · BRIGHTON
RENDEZVOUS PARK SITE

Common Stock—Par Value $25.00—Price $15.00

Send in your subscription at once, using the blank printed below. Subscriptions will be accepted in order of receipt. Make your check payable to the Commerce Trust Company, Trustee, Baltimore, Md., and mail direct to Paul Cleland.

SUBSCRIPTION BOOKS will remain open till noon, June 1st, unless the stock is fully subscribed before that time. Subscriptions will be accepted in the order of their receipt, and the right is reserved to return all remittances received after the stock has been fully subscribed.

SUBSCRIPTION BLANK

.... 1920

MR. PAUL CLELAND,
Law Bldg., Atlantic City, New Jersey
Dear Sir:

I hereby agree to purchase .... shares of the capital stock of The Boardwalk Park Company, of the par value of Twenty-five Dollars ($25.00) per share, at the price of Fifteen Dollars ($15.00) per share and deliver to you herewith my check to the order of the Commerce Trust Company, Trustee, Baltimore Md., in payment therefor.

Very truly yours,

Name ....

Street .... City .... State ....
Y-D

Newspaper Ads Lead to Successful Rendezvous Capital Raise

THE STORY OF TORCHIA HILL

Henry Andrew Torchia, Esq., and Lt. USN (retired)

(Courtesy of Michael Torchia)

THE STORY OF TORCHIA HILL

Brothers Meet in Europe

Two brothers, Staff Sgt. Columbus M. Torchia and Cpl. Felice A. Torchia, Jr., sons of Mr. and Mrs. F. A. Torchia, 1400 Vernon street, met in Holland June 5, after a long separation.

Sgt. Columbus Torchia is serving with the Ninth Army and Cpl. Felice Torchia is with the Fifteenth Army.

They have two other brothers in service, Lt. Henry Torchia, USN, and Sgt. William Torchia, USN.

"Torchia Brothers Meet in Europe"

Amidst the backdrop of war, four weeks after VE Day, with thousands of Allied Forces still engaged in the Far East, the wartime newspaper article offered few details into the meeting, merely confirming its occurrence.[65] It was Michael Torchia, son of Meade, who filled in the missing pieces, shedding light on the event.[66] Staff Sgt. Amedeo "Meade" Columbus Torchia, driven by his Catholic faith, attended church during a time when people were expressing gratitude and earnest prayers for a swift end to the war. Meade sought solace within the sacred confines of the church, offering heartfelt prayers not only for the welfare of his fellow soldiers but also for his own flesh and blood - his three biological brothers who were still actively involved in the ongoing conflict. It was here, in this church and at this time, that Meade would by happenstance reunite with his youngest brother, Felica "Phil" A. Torchia Jr.

The random encounter of these brothers amidst the turmoil of war became an enduring tale that was passed down through subsequent generations of Torchias. This remarkable story not only symbolized the strength of Torchia family bonds, but also emphasized the essence of unity within the family. It was a third brother, Henry Torchia, who conceived the idea of keeping the family united as a tightly knit community.

Born in West Virginia and raised with his siblings in Harrisburg, Henry Torchia was the son of Felice Antonio "Tony" Torchia, Sr. and his wife Catarina. An attorney by trade, Henry was educated at Dickinson College in Pennsylvania and later at the University of Pittsburgh.

Seeking a quieter place to raise his family, away from the congestion of Harrisburg, Henry urged his brothers to embark on a fresh start in rural York County, Pennsylvania. Enchanted by the serene surroundings, where the air was crisp and life much simpler, Henry saw it as an ideal setting to nurture their growing families. In the year 1946, just ten months after the conclusion of World War II, Henry and his wife Pearl made the decision to acquire property on a picturesque hilltop adjacent to Silver Lake, owned by the Silver Lake Improvement Company.

Almost 20 years had elapsed since William G. and Mary A. Stonesifer sold the very first subdivided lot on Silver Lake, and nearly 15 years had passed since the Silver Lake Improvement Company began selling the remaining lots. The "hill" lots, without waterfrontage and some without even a view of the lake, were less desirable, as evident in the two decades it took to find buyers. Henry's purchase of the unsold lots in the subdivision aided the Silver Lake Improvement Company in fulfilling its purpose of disposing of the remaining lots. Recognizing that Henry was looking for land on behalf of other family members, other lot owners saw an opportunity to sell their hillside properties to Henry Torchia. Throughout subsequent real estate transactions, Henry and Pearl acquired eight numbered subdivision lots and three unnumbered parcels from various sellers, including the Silver Lake Improvement Company and its lots 3, 10, 11, and 12.[67]

The Torchia homes, unlike the cottages found on the edge of the lake, were intended for full-time residency, and after the initial use of outhouses, they were equipped with

Some of the Post-War Baby Boom at Torchia Hill, 1950s (Courtesy of Michael Torchia)

proper sanitation. (Even today, Michael Torchia mentions that he "measures wealth" by the number of indoor bathrooms a house has.) Lake cottages were primarily occupied by summer residents, opening on Memorial Day and, in the local vernacular, "shut" on Labor Day. Some residents would only stay for a week or two or visit on weekends. In contrast, the Torchia homes were specifically designed to serve as permanent residences.

Henry and Pearl, accompanied by their son, Henry Andrew "Andy" Jr., and Henry's brother William Aquino "Queenie" and his wife, Kay, moved to the hill, along with their children. Meade, another brother, and his wife, Carmen, also made the move. Regular visitors included the children's paternal grandfather, Tony (the F.A. Torchia from the newspaper article), who would hunt in the surrounding fields. Another frequent visitor was Michael's maternal grandfather, John Scopelliti, who happened to be the father of both Kay and Carmen. (It's worth noting that two Torchia brothers married two Scopelliti sisters, exemplifying how these families looked out for one another.) John Scopelliti would drive down from Williamsport, Pennsylvania to build a house for Queenie and Kay. And it was in this new location, soon to be known as Torchia Hill, that Meade and Carmen welcomed their newborn son, Michael Torchia.

Michael's first steps, with his dad by his side. (Courtesy of Michael Torchia)

Despite being an only child, Michael had the advantage of having five cousins around, forming a ready-made "gang." They always found plenty of activities to keep themselves occupied. They would play shuffleboard at cousin Andy's, construct forts in the dry race bed, swing from vines, and soar out and over Silver Lake Road, much to the dismay of oncoming motorists who would respond with scolding and shaking fists. Andy would playfully encourage the younger cousins to gather behind an outdoor fireplace for a moment of prayer. He'd tell them that candy from heaven would be their reward, then toss penny candy from the L.H. Gross store high into the air, creating a joyful rain of treats for the younger children. The Torchia children chronicled neighborhood events in the 'Silver Lake News' – a very grown-up endeavor involving reporting, typesetting, selling ads, and managing subscriptions that kept the cousins busy for hours and days. And, of course, there was the lake where they could swim, fish, and go boating. When the lake froze over, they eagerly laced up their skates for ice skating with the family and also played spirited games of hockey.

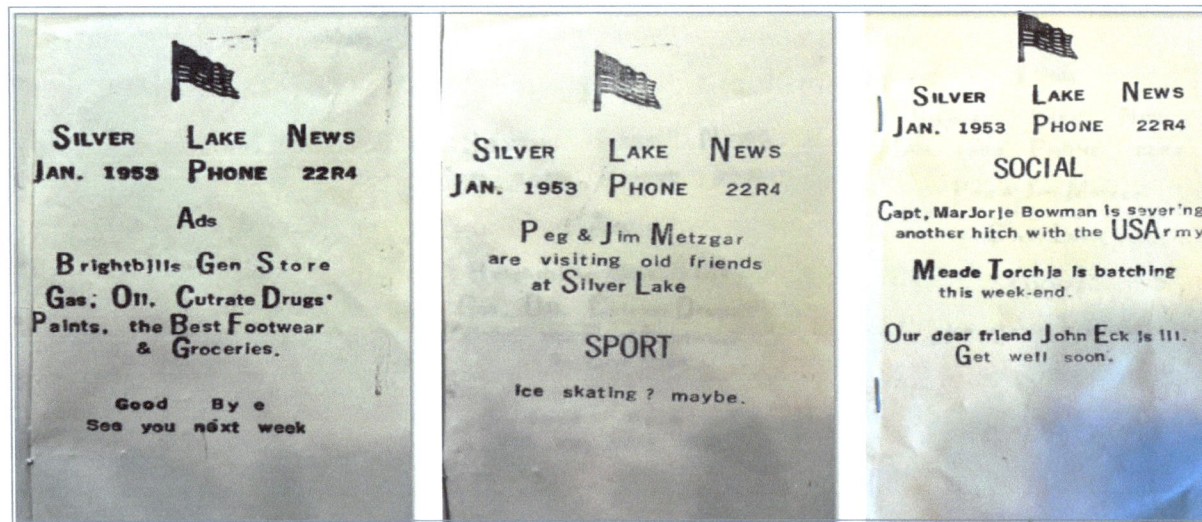

The 'Silver Lake News' captures the events of the week at Silver Lake
(Courtesy of H. Andrew Torchia, Jr.)

The frozen charm of Silver Lake brings smiles to the Torchia and Scopelliti women
(Courtesy of Michael Torchia)

The Silver Lake Community Association consisted of property owners located on or adjacent to the shores of Silver Lake. Membership in the association was voluntary and extended to residents on the hill as well. The annual dues, paid on a voluntary basis, amounted to $15 per year in the 1960's. As Michael recalls, and as others also remember, the $15 fee was primarily allocated to an insurance policy that would provide coverage for any expenses in the event of a child being injured while playing on the lake. As depicted on the SLCA's 1970's map on the left, the entire eastern side of the hill was simply labeled as "Torchia."[68]

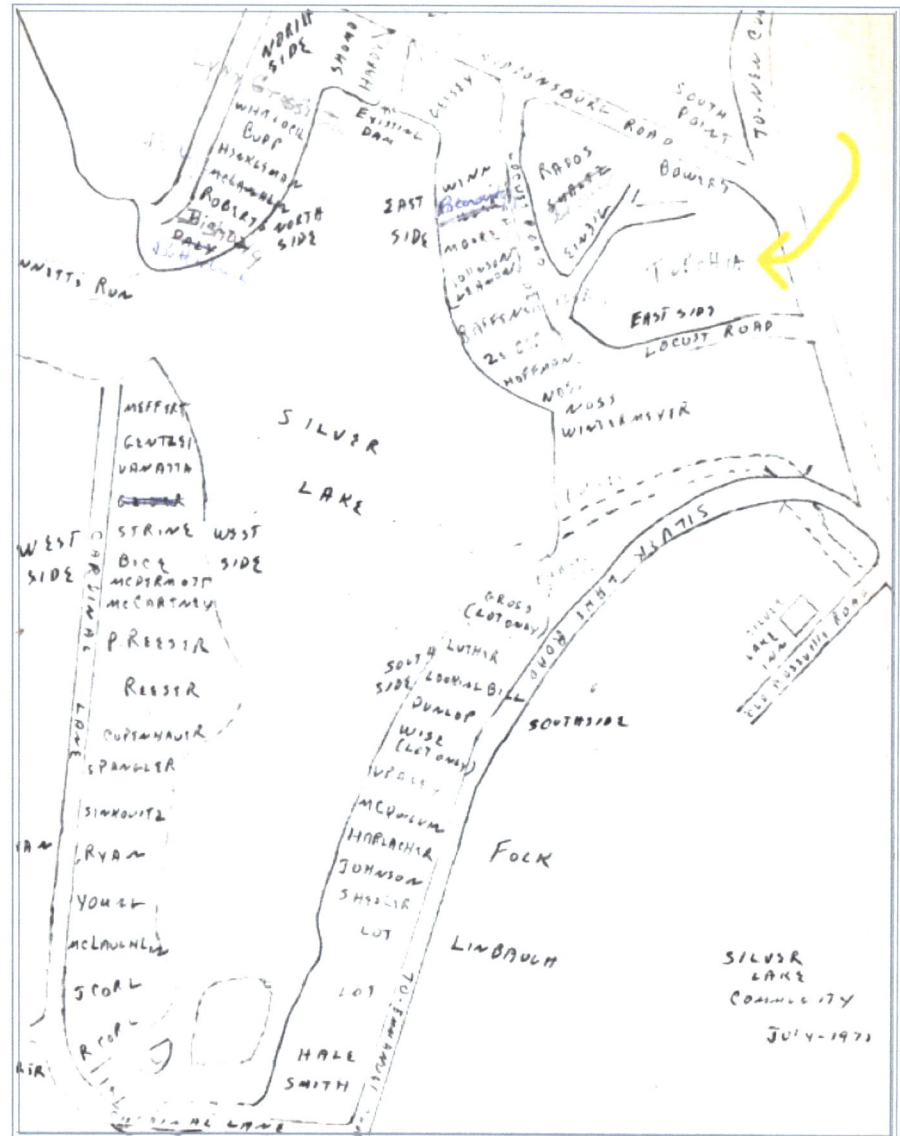

Mapping the Neighborhood: A Hand-Drawn Map of Silver Lake and Torchia Hill (Courtesy of Lee Margot)

Michael, the youngest, watched as his older cousins made their way to the South Point Schoolhouse on Siddonsburg Road, located on the other side of the Silver Lake hill. The walk to school was an easy downhill stroll, but the real challenge came when they had to climb back up the hill. On snowy days, however, they transformed their school-bound journey into a fun adventure by sliding down on their bottoms, covering the 100-yard distance with excitement. Their distinctive method of descending earned them the playful nickname "otters" due to their resemblance to... well, otters.

The eldest Torchia cousins, students at the school, took on the daily responsibility of starting and tending a fire in the coal stove that provided warmth in the old one-room schoolhouse. This task was essential to ensure their teacher, Mrs. Effie Snyder, and their fellow students had a comfortable environment throughout the day. Soon, it would be Michael's turn to attend the school, slide down the snowy hill, and assume the responsibility of tending to the coal stove. However, to his disappointment, the school closed permanently and was sold at public auction in 1955 during the York County school consolidations of the 1950s.[69]

Before long, however, the Torchia families began to move on, and eventually, Michael became the sole cousin remaining on the hill. As his cousin Kathy remarked, being the only one left, poor Michael had to play both the Cowboy and the Indian.[70] Despite being the last Torchia, Michael never felt lonely. There were other children living nearby with whom he spent time, including racing their mini-bikes across East Hill Street and West Hill Street.

In the mid-1990s, now Dr. Michael Torchia was tasked with selling off the remaining Torchia family properties. In June 2023, after a quarter century, Michael returned to the hill properties for the first time, bringing his wife Marge along to share in the sentimental journey. Old friends warmly welcomed them, opening their homes to reminisce about the work of the Torchia and Scopelliti families. However, one thing was missing—the "Esquire," a primitive garage that once housed an old wood and canvas kayak, shelves of law books, and chairs where the men would retreat when chased away by the women folk.

Standing at the intersection of Hill Street and North Avenue, Michael surveyed the now-vacant lot. One neighbor from the Torchia days, Brenda Smiley, unaware of grown-up Michael's identity, came out to see what the commotion was about. In a lighthearted Central Pennsylvania tradition, Michael, recognizing Brenda, playfully put her on the spot, wearing a smile on his face, and challenged her by asking, "Do you remember me?" Understanding the local custom, Brenda realized the result would be the joyful surprise of

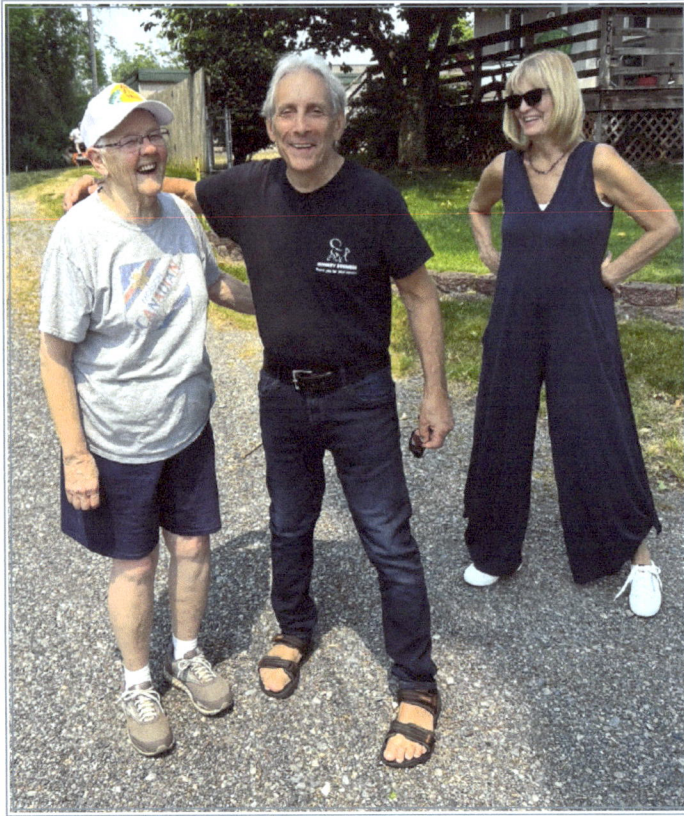

Unexpected and Heartwarming Reunion: Hill Street Neighbors
Reconnect After 30 Years (Authors' Photograph)

rediscovering a long-lost acquaintance. In the photograph on the left, she was rewarded with that joyful memory.

In the end, had the Torchia brothers truly found a simpler life for themselves and their family? Meade made genuine friendships with two locals known as Beaver and Hushpuppy, always ready to lend each other a helping hand. One day, Meade was driving Hushpuppy to a medical appointment and stayed with him in the waiting room. When medical staff entered and called out Hushpuppy's given name, he didn't even recognize his own name. Their friendship, though unsophisticated, remained authentic. In this place, Torchia families would gather, bringing out folding chairs to the edges of their properties, savoring beer, sharing stories, and laughing while the children chased fireflies. Growing up here, the children learned invaluable traits—self-reliance, confidence, and humility—forming bonds that transcended social status. This was a place where Doc H.C. Hetrick would walk down West Street and up the hill to tend to a sick child, charging a mere dollar. Here Michael learned life's profound lessons: to treat everyone with equality and to cherish those who surrounded him.

THE STONE WALLS OF SILVER LAKE

Vibrant greens against the characteristic red stone are striking (Authors' Photograph)

THE STONE WALLS OF SILVER LAKE

As passersby make their way along West Street, on Silver Lake's eastern shoreline, they are greeted by beautiful, hand-crafted, stone walls. These walls act as a retaining wall along West Street and line the spillway overflow channel. They are masterfully constructed using reddish-brown stones in a variety of shapes. They seamlessly blend utilitarian functionality with undeniable aesthetic charm.

In addition to their unique red/brown color, these walls feature pointed coping stones that serve multiple purposes. These stones are both ornamental and functional, redirecting moisture from the top of the wall, particularly during snowfalls. The coping stones remain exposed through moderate snow depth, allowing them to absorb sunlight and warmth, thereby speeding up the melting and evaporation of snow. Furthermore, their design discourages loitering as sitting on the wall is uncomfortable. They act as an effective barrier to deter unwanted trespassers.

The stone employed at the entrance of the Silver Lake summer colony is the renowned 'Brownstone,' sourced from a band of Triassic sandstone running parallel to the Appalachians, extending from Nova Scotia to North Carolina.[71] The decision to use brownstone for the Wiliam G. Stonesifer subdivision's entrance and spillway was likely deliberate, with the goal of instilling a sense of elegance and making a lasting impression on prospective buyers and investors who intended to become seasonal residents or landlords renting out their cottages. The stonemason who constructed these walls remains unknown today, remembered only by his distinctive flowing white beard.

Beauty and function along the spillway discharge channel
(Authors' Photograph)

Redland Sand/Siltstone Walls Guarding the Spillway
Overflow Channel (Authors' Photograph)

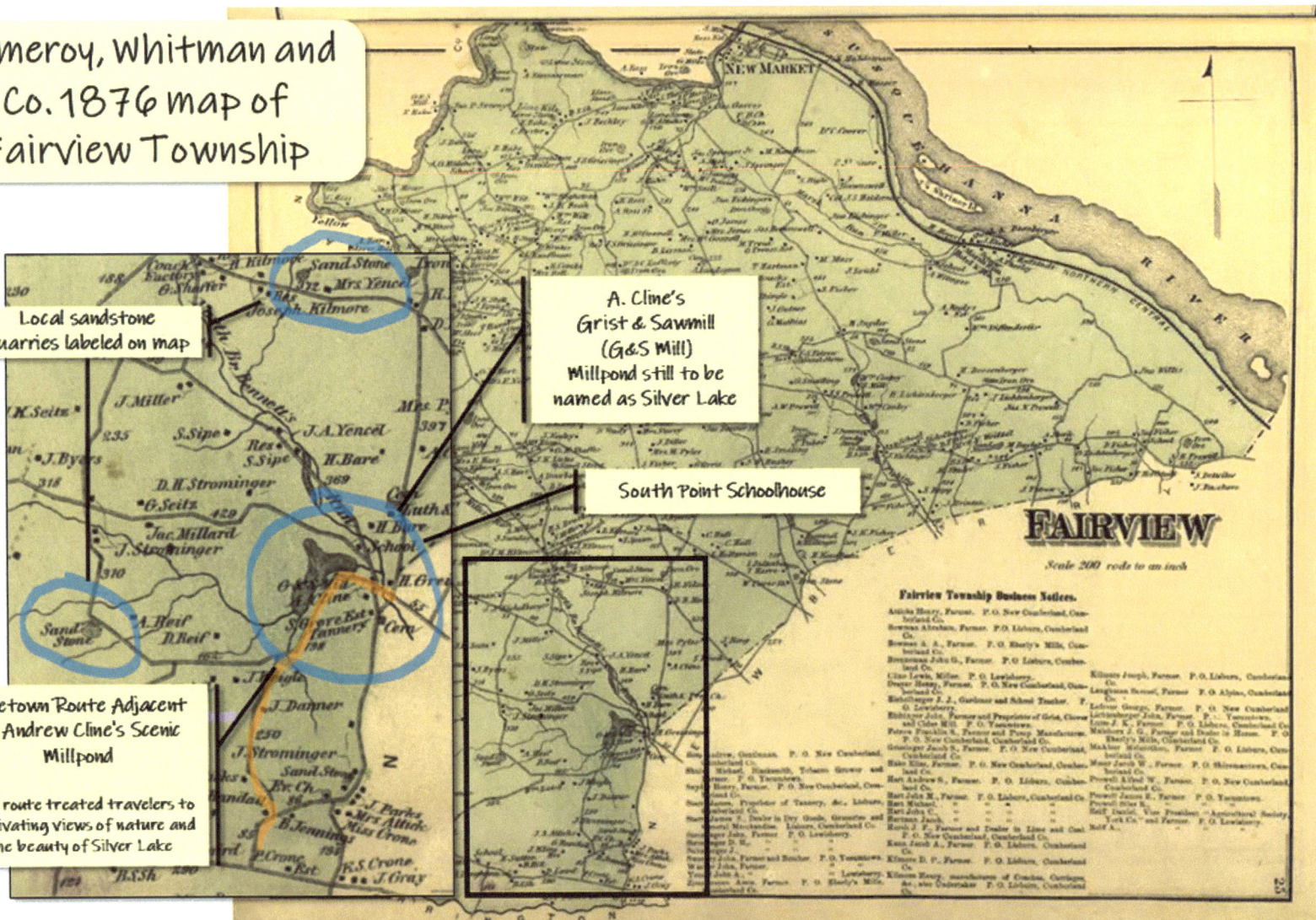

Pomeroy, Whitman and Co. 1876 map of Fairview Township

Local sandstone quarries labeled on map

A. Cline's Grist & Sawmill (G&S Mill) Millpond still to be named as Silver Lake

South Point Schoolhouse

Pinetown Route Adjacent to Andrew Cline's Scenic Millpond

This route treated travelers to captivating views of nature and the beauty of Silver Lake

Historical Mapping: 1876 Pomeroy, Whitman and Co. depiction of Fairview Township, highlighting sandstone quarries, routes west of Lewisberry, and Andrew Clines' millpond (York County History Center)

Exposed coping stones absorb
sunlight, hastening snow's retreat
(Authors' Photograph)

The walls were constructed during the early stages of road development to support the establishment of the summer colony. These walls showcase the locally sourced Redland Sand/Siltstone, known as the 'Gettysburg formation' in geological terms and referred to as 'Brownstone' by builders.[72] This stone was a prevalent choice for construction in the era, highly valued by builders in the late nineteenth and early twentieth centuries for its versatility and quality. The stone's distinct color and unique properties enabled the creation of remarkable buildings and structures. (Triassic brownstone, known as "freestone," is durable yet easily carved and shaped. It exhibits a variety of hues such as gray, blue, pink, or purple.) The stones were most likely mined from one of the many quarries in York County. The highlighted areas on the 1876 Pomeroy, Whitman, and Co. map of Fairview Township[73] indicate the presence of sandstone deposits within Fairview Township, along with the location of the Andrew Cline grist and sawmill (G&S Mill A. Cline) and its associated millpond, which is now known as Silver Lake.

Mason's Mark: Advertisements Carved in Stone
(Authors' Photograph)

A variety of local structures in the vicinity of Silver Lake showcase the use of this stone, including the Lewisberry Mills, its adjacent house, the Jacob and Christina Kaufman mansion, the South Point Schoolhouse, the Quaker Meeting Houses, and numerous homes in Lewisberry. Additionally, stone foundations are prevalent in various constructions like barns, residences, and cottages around Silver Lake, highlighting the significance of stone masonry as a coveted and indispensable skill. Some masons, like Samuel Knisley, inscribed their names and achievements on buildings they constructed, such as the cornerstone of John Harmon's mill. Similarly, Joel Willis, a mason, left his mark on Jacob and Christina Kaufman's brownstone mansion in 1812.

Early settlers who aimed to construct larger two and two and a half story stone buildings often depended on the indigenous Susquehannock people to transport and stack the heavy stones along the edges of walls that were many feet off the ground.

Against the backdrop of Silver Lake, these walls symbolize the enduring spirit of this place. They stand as a reminder of both their aesthetic appeal and the rich history they represent.

Redland Friends (Quakers) Meeting House Crafted
from Beautiful Brownstone (Authors' Photograph)

LOG HAVEN: THE HENKELMANN FAMILY RETREAT

Winter's Embrace: Silver Lake's snowy blanket envelops Henkelmann's Log Haven in peaceful isolation (Authors' Photograph)

LOG HAVEN: THE HENKELMANN FAMILY RETREAT

As boaters and swimmers head towards Silver Lake's north shore, they come across a pleasant sight—a row of charming cottages lining the water's edge. Set back a bit from the shore, and shaded by oak trees, one finds a rustic log cabin that blends in naturally with its surroundings, as if it has always been there. The weathered logs of the cabin hint at its history and character, creating a serene and peaceful atmosphere that feels timeless. Observers can't help but wonder about the stories held within its walls and how this log cabin found its place by the lake.

Vintage Charm: An Old Log Cabin Nestled Among Silver Lake's Towering Trees (Authors' Photograph)

A Family Portrait Featuring Gottfried and Wilhelmina Henkelmann, with Young Reinhold Seated on the Right

A Life of Faith and Duty: Rev. Reinhold Henkelman,
Moravian Minister, and U.S. Army Chaplain
(Courtesy of Lee Margot)

Gottfried Henkelmann was born in Poland in 1855. In the 1870s, fleeing religious persecution, he moved with his family to Russia, where he met and married Wilhelmina Moller. Together, they had eight children including Reinhold. During his time in the Russian army, Gottfried acquired medical knowledge and language skills, becoming fluent in Russian, German, Polish, and later English.[74]

In 1897, again seeking religious freedom, Gottfried, Wilhelmina, and their children left Russia and settled in Alberta, Canada, where they joined the Bruederfeld Moravian Church. In 1902, in Bethlehem, Pennsylvania, Gottfried was ordained as a Moravian minister.

Gottfried instilled his passions, purpose, and skills, including his proficiency in multiple languages and woodworking, in his son Reinhold, born in 1893. Reinhold and his wife Caroline raised their family in the United States – sons Charles (a future doctor) and David (a future reverend). Following his father's path, Reinhold became a Moravian minister, and was a long-time pastor of the First Moravian Church in York County, Pennsylvania, carrying on the family's legacy of service and dedication.[75]

> Being the whole of Lot No. 8 and one-half of Lot No. 7 as laid out on a plan of lots of Silver Lake.
>
> Being part of the same tract of land which Wm. G. Stonesifer and Mary A. Stonesifer, his wife, by their deed dated the 27th day of July, A. D. 1931, did grant and convey unto the Silver Lake Improvement Company, and also the same tract of land which Elmer E. Strominger (single man) by his deed dated May 7th, 1940, did grant and convey unto the Silver Lake Improvement Company.

Unveiling the Land Legacy: A Deed Excerpt Revealing the
Origins of Marie Ave's Spacious Lots

Edgar and Annie Wantz, members of the church and owners of one of only four cabins on Marie Avenue, invited the Henkelmanns to their summer cabin on Silver Lake. Upon discovering the lake-front lots still available at Silver Lake, Rev. Reinhold Henkelmann entered into a purchase arrangement in 1938 with SLIC, to secure land for his use. The specific financial details have been lost to time. Finally, on June 15, 1940, he settled on the lot and the deed was recorded.[76] To form this lot, the Silver Lake Improvement Company acquired a 70-ft section of land from E. E. Strominger for $187.50. This section of land was situated between Marie Avenue and the land already owned by the Silver Lake Improvement Company from their previous purchase of land from William G. Stonesifer. (E.E. Strominger was an initial investor in the Silver Lake Improvement Company and collaborated with the company on the sale of later lots, owning the land to the west of the William G. Stonesifer purchase.)

Following the E.E. Strominger acquisition, the Silver Lake Improvement Company took the initiative to divide Lot No. 7 in half and combine it with Lot No. 8, effectively expanding the future Henkelmann's lot's width from 50 ft to 75 ft. Consequently, this enlargement extended the available lot from its original size, which was roughly 50 ft by 80 ft, to a more substantial 75 ft by 150 ft. (The transformation of the properties by consolidating Strominger and what once was Stonesifer lands into larger lots is best seen in the image to the right, particularly with the unsold Lot No. 15.)[77] By 1940, 13 years after the sale of the first lake community property, waterfront lots were selling for more than $1, as Rev. Henkelmann paid $375.

Ministers generally live in the church parsonages of the congregations they serve, rarely owning their own home. Right from the beginning, Caroline had her heart set on a log cabin. While the family saved up for it, they decided to build and live in a garage. Half of the space served as a functional garage and workshop, while the other half became their living area. There were designated sleeping spots, and a basic "kitchen" was arranged in one corner, equipped with a sink, cupboard, grey icebox, and

1931 Lot Plan: 'South Side of Silver Lake, Fairview Township, York Co., Penna.' [Recorded in 1947] - Please Note: The Direction 'South' Should Be Corrected to 'North' due to an error in reporting at the county recorder's office

two "hot plates." These hot plates also heated water for their Saturday night baths. An outhouse was also included in the setup. To access drinking water, a kind neighbor allowed them to use their outdoor pump since it would take a year to establish a Henkelmann water source. Furthermore, a small caravan trailer, frequently used for trips to Canada, was parked on the site where the family hoped to eventually build their log cabin, reserving the space until its construction. [78]

While driving one day, Reinhold noticed a sign that read, "LOGS FOR SALE." Intrigued, he turned onto a side road and discovered a substantial pile of logs beside a newly built brick house. Upon speaking to the owner, Reinhold learned that the owner had initially intended to construct a log cabin-style home, but his wife's preference had shifted towards a brick house. Recognizing the opportunity, Rev. Henkelmann swiftly negotiated a deal, purchasing the log cabin kit for $200. In

Where It All Began: The Henkelmann Log Cabin in a Clearing (Courtesy of Lee Margot)

the process, he also became aware of an elderly man nearby who was renowned for his expertise in log cabin construction - the master craftsman was 84 years old, and his assistant was 78. With their skilled hands at work, and aided by Rev. Henkelmann's parishioners, the vision of "Log Haven" started to take shape.

Living by the lake ushered in immediate adventures for the young family, starting with fishing and enjoying the week's catch for dinner. There were "Mud Battles Royale" with silt from the lake's bottom as an ample supply of ammunition, and one memorable incident involved the frantic search for a visitor's

glass eyeball that had popped out and fallen into the water.

Winter brought opportunities to entertain Canadian nephews who arrived at "Uncle Reinys" for the holidays and the hoped-for ice on the lake. Uncle David, also known as Reverend David Henkelmann, and continuing the legacy of ministry, fondly recalled, "During my college years, I would invite the Pre-Theological fraternity to the cabin for a weekend. Once a roaring fire was lit, most of us would plunge into the lake for a bracing polar bear dip...and then hurry out as quickly as possible!"

Thirteen years later, with dense treetop canopies and grandchildren beginning to arrive at Reinhold's and Caroline's—now Grandpa and Mimi—log cabin, future generations were poised for Silver Lake adventures. Their son, Charles, a pioneer in nuclear medicine in the U.S. Navy, and his wife Helen Sturdevant, a trained singer and member of the Oratorio Society of New York, called San Diego, California, their home. Their expertise and skills led them on journeys around the world, carrying on the family's legacy of service. Charles and Helen were blessed with three children: Lee (born in New York), Holly (born in Panama), and Todd (born in California).

Lee recalls the ship voyage to Panama, during which one of the crew members crafted a makeshift harness with a leash, securely fastened to three-year-old Lee. This precaution was taken to ensure her mother could hold on to her and keep her safe during the journey.

As the grandchildren grew, and their parents traveled, the children eagerly anticipated being dropped off for the summer at Grandpa's and Mimi's log cabin – a place that had become their cherished summer home. This annual tradition thrilled them, offering the perfect opportunity to learn swimming, fishing, and boating. With Grandpa's patient and accommodating nature, he would skillfully clean the little perch caught by the grandchildren – a two-bite fillet – while Mimi would cook them up into a special treat fit for royalty. The lake area was bustling with plenty of other children, providing them with endless playmates and opportunities for adventurous escapades.

The children made lifelong memories exploring the woods, engaging in their own form of gymnastics by balancing across fallen trees, and building forts in the mostly dry mill race. Just like the Torchia children, they would surprise passing drivers on Silver Lake Road with their playful antics. Lee fondly recalls that, back then, the lake had slightly submerged tree stumps. She would swim out to them and stand on top, making the water appear shallow. Mischievously, she would signal her friends to join her, only to laugh at their surprise when realizing they were walking out into deeper waters.

When it was time for Mom and Dad to arrive and pick them up for the return trip to California, Lee fondly recalls taking the canoe out as a family. Moving the canoe required a team effort to maneuver the heavy wood and canvas vessel into the water. As the family glided across the serene waters of Silver Lake, her mother Helen's beautiful voice would fill the air with melodic tunes, singing about lakes, forests, sky, and moon. Her songs added to the enchantment of the surroundings, making it a truly memorable and magical experience.

Christmas was a cherished time for the Henkelmann family. Three generations of Henkelmanns would study and be ordained at the Bethlehem Moravian Seminary. Rev. Reinhold Henkelmann delivered his Christmas Eve Vigil Service sermon annually at Bethlehem's Central Moravian Church with all available family in attendance.

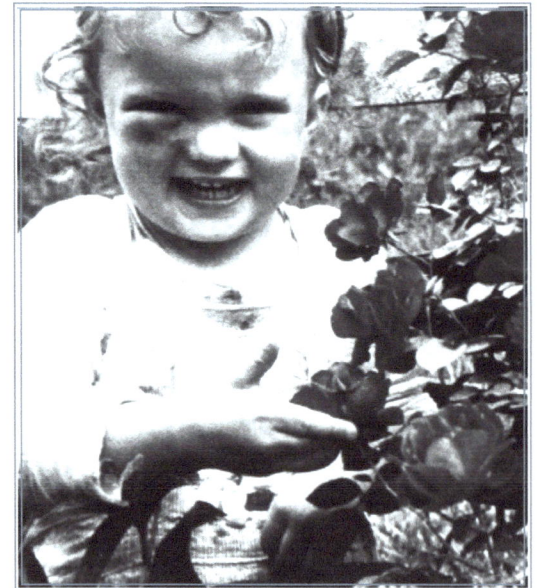

Already a world traveler, three-year-old Lee's favorite destination is Grandpa and Mimi's log cabin (Courtesy of Lee Margot)

Family Heritage on Display: Lee Margot Offers a Heartfelt Welcome from the Log Cabin
(Authors' Photograph)

Returning to the Silver Lake at two in the morning, the fireplace would be lit and a joyous gathering at the log cabin would begin. Upon arrival, the children were sent up to the cabin loft, the warmest spot in the home. Lee and her siblings would listen to the crackling of the fire and the adults' conversations as they decorated the Christmas tree, adding to the cozy and memorable atmosphere.

The cabin is adorned with vintage furnishings, handmade quilts, and the hand-crafted stone fireplace. The walls are decorated with photographs along with curious artifacts. Each item holds a fragment of the past, creating a warm and nostalgic atmosphere.

Back to 1941, at the outbreak of war, 44-year-old Rev. Reinhold Henkelmann made a significant decision and joined the U.S. Army Chaplain Corps serving in seven American Prisoner of War (POW) camps housing German prisoners in Maryland. His language skills in German and Russian were of great value here. Some German prisoners had been detailed to Washington D.C. and, at the outbreak of war, interred in POW camps, while others were from Rommel's African Corps – hardened soldiers and Nazis.[79]

At first, Rev. Henkelmann played the organ, sang German hymns, and delivered his sermons in German to an empty chapel. However, before long, he managed to attract over 300 regular German Army soldiers to attend his services, though the ideologues never joined in. During his sermons and conversations with the prisoners afterward, he often spoke about his place of safety, refuge, and family love – his "Log Haven," his log cabin home on Silver Lake. Undoubtedly, this imagery resonated with the soldiers and connected with memories of Germany itself.

Reinhold found out that one of the German prisoners, who was working as a cook in the Officers Mess, had a talent for wood-carving. This led to the creation of a split log measuring about 2 ½ feet by 8 inches, with the name "Log Haven" carved into it. The letters were beautifully done using colors made from materials found in the kitchen, set against a dark background of shoe polish. The "Log Haven" artifact in the photograph to the right adorns the mantelpiece above the fireplace today.

'Log Haven' Artifact Takes Its Place Above the Fireplace (Authors' Photograph)

Log Haven's Tranquil Dining Space: A Window to Silver Lake's Natural Beauty (Authors' Photograph)

Log Haven, to Reinhold's granddaughter Lee, is more than just a cabin by the lake; it is the very essence of home, where her heart resides. It holds a special place in her soul, a sanctuary of comfort and tranquility where she seeks solace in times of need. The memories of her cherished family moments make it a haven of love and warmth. Even the smallest changes stir a mix of emotions, a reluctance to let go of the past, like refusing to part with Mimi's delicate curtains, now brittle from the years of sunlight. For Lee, Log Haven is timeless, forever etched with love and treasured for all eternity.

While interviewing Lee, we stepped outside, capturing photos of the majestic trees and the breathtaking view across the lake. As we looked around, we observed that each resident believed they had the best view of the lake.

"Yes," Lee said, a playful glint in her eye, followed by a mischievous smile and laughter, "but deep down, we all know that we truly do!"

Lakefront Harmony: Residents Cherish Their Unique Views (Authors' Photograph)

Trumpeter Swan
(Courtesy of Ken Boyer)

© Ken Boyer

SILVER LAKE: A WAYPOINT ON THE AMERICAN ATLANTIC FLYWAY

Canada Geese Photograph
(Courtesy of Ken Boyer)

SILVER LAKE: A WAYPOINT ON THE AMERICAN ATLANTIC FLYWAY

"Tragedy strikes as a construction team devastates a wilderness area near Amy's Canadian home. Amidst the turmoil, Amy discovers an abandoned nest containing 16 goose eggs. In time, these eggs will develop into goslings that are meant to learn important behaviors and migratory routes from their now absent parents, further adding to the predicament. Who will show them the way to fly south to their winter migratory home in North Carolina? With uncertainty looming, Amy and her dad hatch a plan – pun absolutely intended – setting the stage for a compelling drama."

Though this might sound overly dramatic, it's the core plot of the 1996 Colombia Pictures film, "Fly Away Home," which drew inspiration from the real-life experiences of Bill Lishman. Lishman, an ultralight aviator from Canada, connected with Bill Carrick, a naturalist working on imprinting behavior on geese. In 1988, Lishman became the first person to lead the flight of geese with an aircraft, and in 1993, he conducted the first aircraft-led migration of birds.[80]

In the film, Amy's strategy to guide the geese to North Carolina takes them over York County Pennsylvania, passing near Silver Lake. This flight path aligns with the American Atlantic Flyway, a migratory route that extends southward from Canada. Along this route, numerous locations serve as gathering spots for migratory birds, supporting activities like breeding, feeding, or resting during specific intervals. While a few species may spend the entire season at these stopovers, the majority continue their journey.

Ken Boyer, a long-time Silver Lake resident and former hunter, set aside his duck calls and decoys in favor of a camera to capture the visiting birds. He recognized that the variety of bird species at Silver Lake wasn't a random occurrence. He correctly surmised that the lake fell within the migratory flight path known as the Atlantic Flyway. Applying his hunting skills to the realm of photography, Ken wondered, How close can I get to these different waterfowl and raptors to truly capture their beauty? His patient approach pays off, demonstrating that with persistence, he can get remarkably close to his subjects. " This form of photography," he explained, "has become my way of sharing nature's gifts with everyone who appreciates

Nature's Highway: The American Atlantic Flyway
- A Birdwatcher's Dream (Authors' illustration)

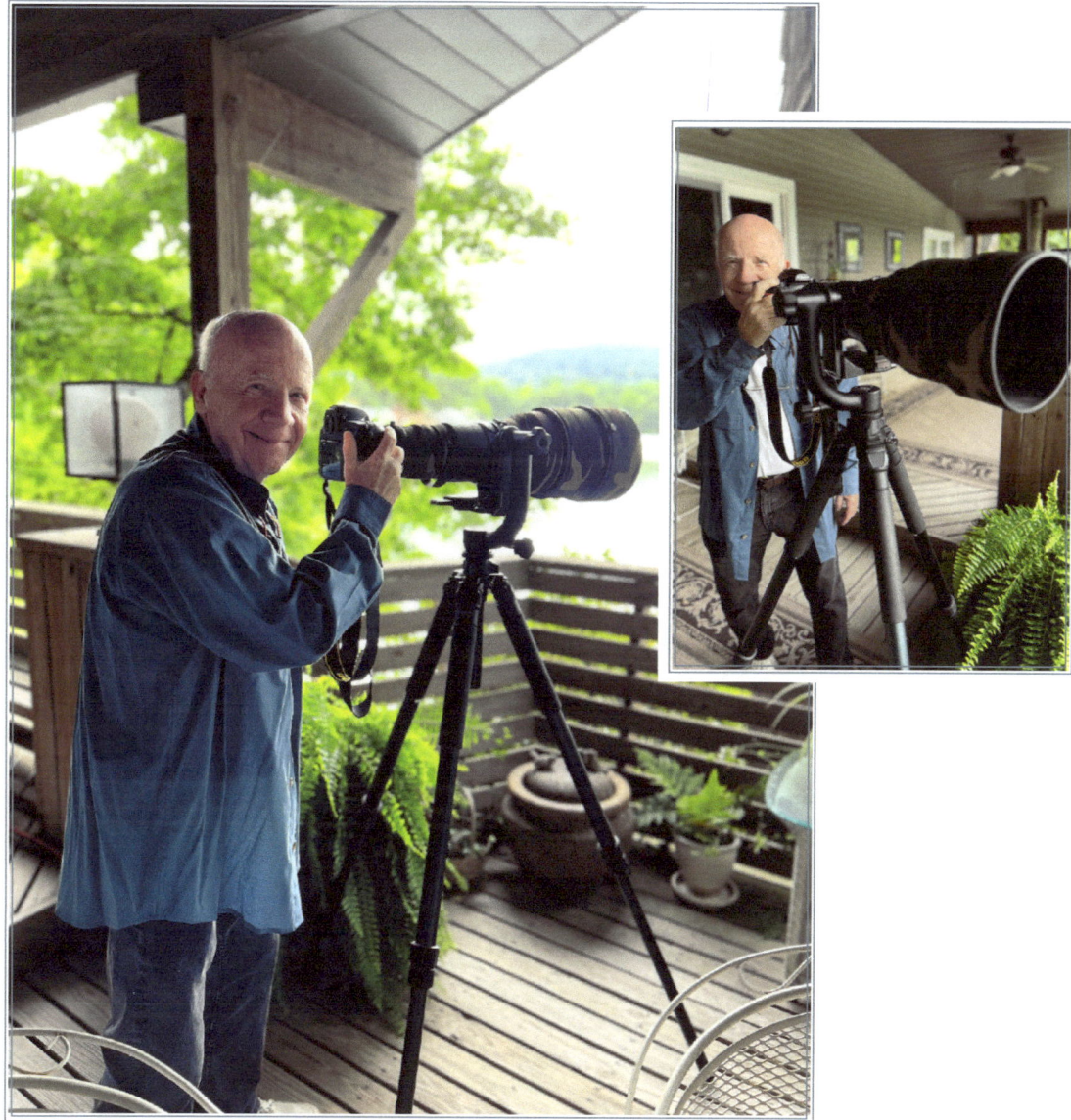

Silver Lake Unveiled: Ken Boyer's Extraordinary Perspective
(Authors' Photograph)

the lake. It allows visitors, residents, and others to experience nature's authentic habitat and its captivating moments."[81]

Silver Lake serves as a migratory sanctuary for a diverse range of waterfowl and raptors. Each year, as spring arrives and autumn sets in, this peaceful haven becomes a bustling center of activity for these magnificent creatures.

In the serene surroundings of Silver Lake, a vibrant display of birdlife unfolds season after season. Great Egrets grace the waters during their spring migration, while the presence of a Great Blue Heron remains steady throughout the year. As the weather cools, Black-crowned Night Herons emerge in the evenings, accompanied by occasional visits from Snowy Egrets and Little Egrets.

The lake's calm waters attract various waterfowl species. From the familiar, year-round, Mallard Ducks to the elusive Hooded Mergansers that arrive in early spring, each species adds its unique charm to Silver Lake's landscape. Swans also grace the skies – from the grace of Mute Swans to the grandeur of Trumpeter Swans, their fleeting appearances add an air of elegance.

Even the skies above Silver Lake contribute to its charm. Raptors take flight, leaving their mark on the sky. Bald Eagles, both residents and travelers, soar overhead, symbolizing freedom. The resounding call of Ospreys fills the air, a reminder of their enduring presence. And on occasion, the sight of Peregrine Falcons invokes awe at nature's mastery of flight.

Within this natural sanctuary, wildlife thrive harmoniously. Herons, egrets, ducks, and hawks coexist, weaving a colorful tapestry that is Silver Lake's ecosystem. As seasons transition and the air carries the promise of new beginnings of spring or the poignant farewell of autumn, this tranquil haven remains timeless.

Silver Lake plays host to both common and rare species. We witness the migratory journeys of countless winged creatures finding comfort and sustenance in this quiet corner of Pennsylvania. With each passing year, Silver Lake remains a stage for the captivating dance of waterfowl and raptors – a reflection of life's eternal cycle and nature's timeless rhythm.

Ken possesses an impressive collection of photographs featuring more than 92 bird species he has captured at Silver Lake. In this book, he generously shares a selection of those images.

Canada Geese: Graceful Arrivals on the American Atlantic Flyway - Silver Lake Stopover
(Courtesy of Ken Boyer)

Great Egret
(Courtesy of Ken Boyer)

Protected Species: Male Old Squaw – Long-tailed Duck
(Courtesy of Ken Boyer)

Great Blue Heron (Courtesy of Ken Boyer)

Beneath the Surface: Underwater Fishing Prowess: Common Loon
(Courtesy of Ken Boyer)

Beneath the Surface: Underwater Fishing Prowess: The protected Horned Grebe (Courtesy of Ken Boyer)

Male Common Merganser (Courtesy of Ken Boyer)

© Ken Boyer

Peregrine Falcon (Courtesy of Ken Boyer)

Male Pileated Woodpecker (Courtesy of Ken Boyer)

Osprey (Courtesy of Ken Boyer)

LINGER LONGER: A MILLER TRADITION

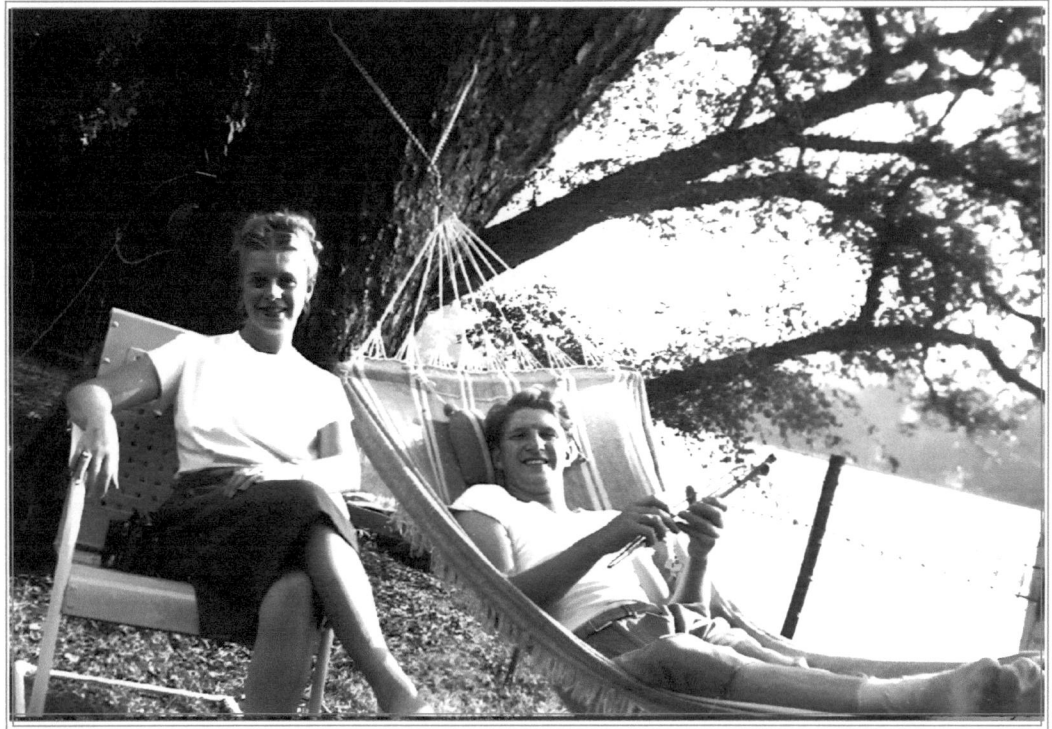

Shirley and Harry: Ringing in joy and music at the cottage
(Courtesy of Gary W. Peck)

LINGER LONGER: A MILLER TRADITION

He was raised on a farm in rural Snyder County, worked as an underground mechanic in the coal mines (even once caught and mangled his left index finger in the gears of an operating machine and completed the amputation one-handed with his pocketknife). Later, as a coal yard proprietor and delivery operator, coal became his livelihood, and in time, it would take his life. But on this date, July 5th, 1945, coal delivered to him his greatest treasure.

William "Bill" Harrison Miller delivered coal to people's homes and dumped it in their basement coal bins, where they would shovel it into a furnace to heat their homes. One day, Bill was delivering coal to Emory Reese in his Warrington Township home, near Dillsburg. Emory was the proprietor of Reese's Variety Store in York. Emory turned to Bill and said, in effect, "Bill, I bought a cottage on Silver Lake a couple of months ago, but my wife refuses to use the outhouse. Now, she wants me to sell the cottage. Are you interested in buying it?"

So, on July 5, 1945, less than two months after the end of the war in Europe and one and a half months before the end of the war in the Pacific, Emory F. Reese and Sallie E. Reese sold their lakefront property – situated between Doc H.C. Hetrick's place and

Making waves and memories from Bill's dock at Silver Lake (Courtesy of Donna Miller Sistek)

C.H. Desenberg's place – to William H. Miller and his wife, Florence Matter Miller. Tenants in Harrisburg their entire lives, this was the only property they ever owned.

Bill had acquired lakefront property, typically priced beyond the means of a coal deliverer, and he took immediate advantage of its appeal to reunite and reconnect with his numerous brothers and sisters (and in-laws) —Bill and Florence each had eight siblings. This land also embodied the attributes that LeGrand Dutcher and C.L. McKenzie had sought for their Silver Lake Incorporated amusement park: a tranquil lake for communing with nature, a spot for picnics, swimming, fishing, and boating. It even featured a kind of amusement ride—a rope swing hanging from the tree slanted over the lake. Children would eagerly use the rope swing, engaging in a display of acrobatics and joyful abandon as they reached the ideal height and released the rope, dropping into the lake water

Fueling up for a picturesque canoe trip across Silver Lake (Courtesy of Gary W. Peck)

below.

"Linger Longer," as Bill named his retreat, operated as a seasonal cottage, welcoming guests from Memorial Day through Labor Day. During the colder months, from October through April, Bill was busy with coal deliveries. Despite his demanding workweek, he still found time to visit the cottage on weekends. There, he indulged in his love for his cottage, pursuing activities like boating and fishing. (Bringing back memories of his youth, Florence would fry catfish eggs for Bill's breakfast that he had harvested from his morning catch.) He also dedicated time to hands-on main-

tenance tasks, such as house painting, building an outdoor fireplace, and working on the flatbottomed boat's White Motor Co. outboard motor, notable to his grandsons for its pull-cord starter. He also dedicated his time and effort to the SLCA Dams and Streams Committee of which he was a member, responsible for "handling all matters pertaining to the dams and streams of the lake." Of course, there was always time for relaxation with a Rolling Rock beer! Florence generally kept him confined to the garage for those libations, but not always.

The cottage held a special place in Florence's heart, providing her with a cherished venue to host her various ladies' clubs. She was a sociable "joiner" and actively involved in numerous clubs and organizations in Harrisburg. Upon acquiring the cottage, Florence enthusiastically assumed the role of social coordinator, regularly inviting fellow organization members to join her there. Few declined her summer

Coffee, company, and Silver Lake's serenity – a perfect blend! (Courtesy of Gary W. Peck)

invitations, as the visits offered a welcome escape from the urban heat, making it a much-loved gathering spot for socializing amid the backdrop of nature.

During the weekends, the cottage became a lively hub of family activity. Bill and Florence understood the importance of close-knit family relationships, learned during their upbringing in the late 1800s and early 1900s in the countryside. Back in those days, there were no televisions, radios, or movie theaters to provide entertainment; instead, society was your own family. As life progressed, siblings got married or moved away. A few decades later, the cottage would become a place for them to come together once more, recapturing the lightheartedness of their youth.

Family gatherings were where deep familial relationships were nurtured. Laughter, jokes, and playful antics were not just encouraged but celebrated as a way to entertain one another. Over the years, these bonds grew stronger, and by the time Bill purchased the cottage, four decades of family connections meant that visitors could truly let their hair down and savor life.

Returning to the countryside meant a return to the familiar activities of their rural youth. Days were filled with fishing, boating, and swimming, enjoyed by all. As night fell, card games of all kinds came out, accompanied by sisters sharing stories about their brothers that never failed to make everyone laugh.

And then, there was the food. Delicious Pennsylvania Dutch

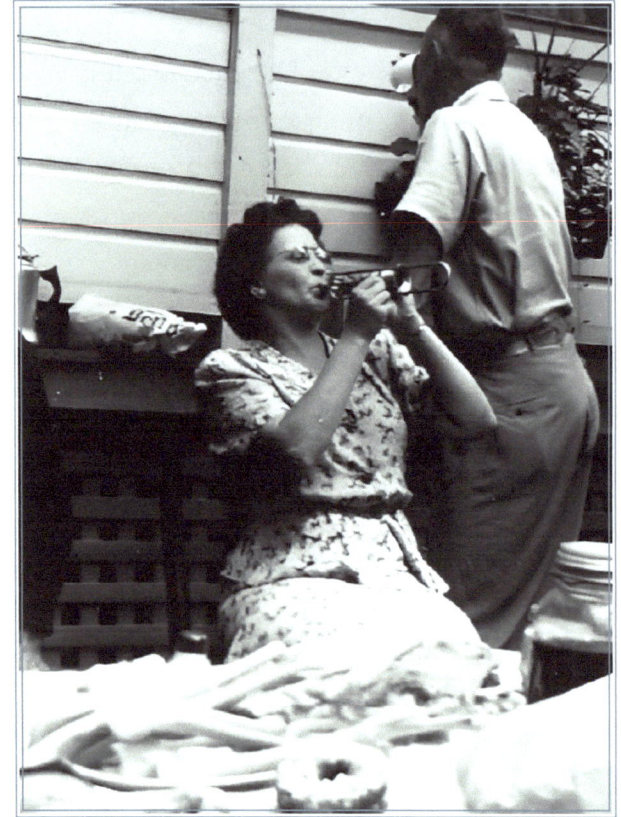

Bill and Florence's feast: Good food, great company, and a hint of musical whimsy!! (Courtesy of Gary W. Peck)

dishes, crafted by Florence in a shoe box sized 'kitchen' with no running water and only a two-burner stove, complemented by the dishes guests brought with them. She would shop at her favorite city farmers' market, and any items missing from the list were usually reserved for visits to the local farms or a quick trip to LH Gross' local market. Florence

Captured in the moment: A lakeside anniversary celebration at the Linger Longer
(Courtesy of Gary W. Peck)

A scene from yesteryear: Oldsters, makeshift tables, and lakeside
dining serving Pennsylvania Dutch favorites. Red-beet eggs, anyone?
(Courtesy of Donna Miller Sistek)

and sisters, daughters and grandchildren would shell peas, husk corn, peel potatoes etc. on benches outside the cottage. One such bench still sits on the Linger Longer porch today. (LH Gross' was where the children would buy their penny candy—Tootsie Rolls, Bit-O-Honey, Root Beer Barrels, Mary Janes, wax bottles with a little juice in them, candy buttons on paper strips, Jawbreakers, Licorice whips or laces, and candy cigarettes, to name just a few.) Bill purchased a block of ice for the old-style Coca-Cola ice chest, and he would chop it into smaller pieces as soon as they arrived at the cottage to ice down his beer and their favorite sodas: root beer, cream soda, and birch beer. And, of course, gallons of hot coffee were always a must for every gathering!

The small cottage lacked enough space for a sit-down meal, so they would bring out sawhorses from the garage for table legs and remove the two bedroom doors from their hinges for tabletops. This allowed them to create makeshift tables that could seat a dozen or more family members.

The screened-in porch had a glider and a porch swing, but overnight visitors always managed to find sleeping space on the porch for themselves, enjoying the cool mountain air and the joy of being surrounded by family. These weekends at the cottage were more than just get-togethers; they were a celebration of the enduring bonds of family, the simple pleasures of the countryside, and the warmth of shared laughter and love.

From sunset to slumber: Where gliders and swings set the rhythm of
the evening (Courtesy of Donna Miller Sistek)

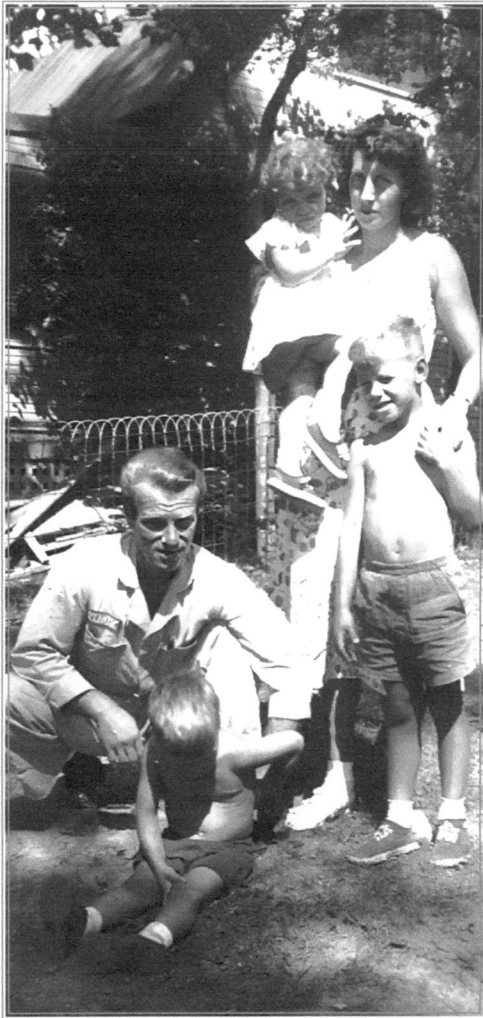

Simple Pleasures by the Lake: Bob and Lilly Miller's family savoring a sunny lakeside escape (Courtesy of Donna Miller Sistek)

In due time, Bill's son Robert, a U.S. Army veteran, along with his German war bride Lilly, and Bill's son-in-law Harry Peck, a U.S. Navy veteran married to daughter Shirley, returned from overseas at the conclusion of World War II. The cottage provided them with a haven as they transitioned back to civilian life, seeking a return to normalcy. Bill and Florence, of Pennsylvania Dutch heritage (with "Dutch" being a variation of the German word "Deutsch," meaning German), and lifelong speakers of a German dialect, played a vital role in helping Lilly, a German speaker, ease into American life.

Soon, the next generation made its entrance, led by Robert Jr. (Bob), born on the Fourth of July, followed by Gary, the son of Harry and Shirley, as well as Bob's siblings, Steve and Donna.

The arrival of grandchildren was a special moment for Bill and Florence, who became affectionately known from that moment on as "Pappy" and "Memmy" to their growing family. Bob, as the first grandchild, quickly became the center of attention, leading to more frequent gatherings at the cottage.

Wash time was never boring with the well pump!
(Courtesy of Gary W. Peck)

Sawhorses were sometimes used as intended - Robert "Bob" Jr. follows in his "Pappy's" footsteps! (Courtesy of Donna Miller Sistek)

Bob recalls, "People were always carrying on. It was a free-for-all; I don't think anybody ever slept."[82] Donna adds, "It felt like Memmy's sisters were there almost every weekend, and every visit was filled with laughter to the point of tears!"[83]

Florence's sisters often enjoyed the lake, either by swimming or taking out a boat. "That boat was as heavy as a battleship," recalls Bob. "It must have been made out of steel. It took six or seven men to lift it out of the water."

Bob remembers, "My Mom had the eye of a photographer. She would borrow other people's cameras and take pictures of everything! I don't know if she ever owned a camera." The abundance of cottage photographs our family has today is a testament to her passion.

Ready to set sail! The flat-bottom boat is ready for family and friends (Courtesy of Gary W. Peck)

Setting sail with a boatload of laughter and friendship on Silver Lake
(Courtesy of Gary W. Peck)

Reaching new heights with friends by the lakeside!
(Courtesy of Donna Miller Sistek)

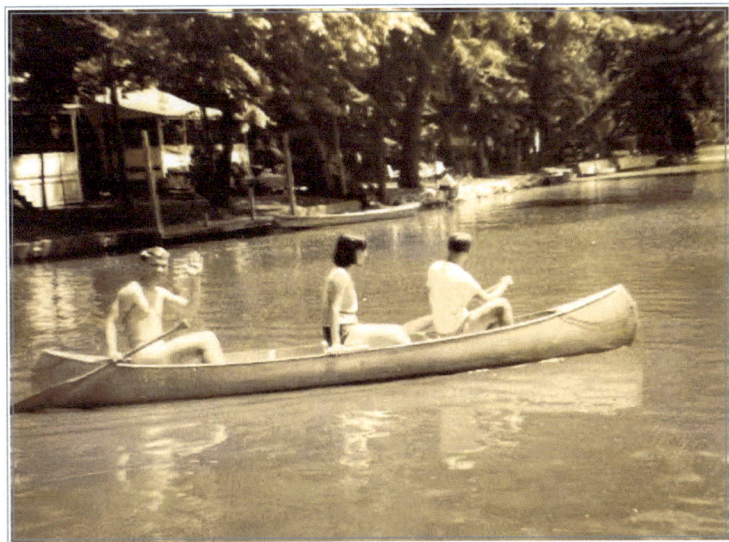

Boy in canoe waving- friendship on Silver Lake
(Courtesy of Donna Miller Sistek)

In 1966, Bob hosted his high school graduation party, and the cottage and the lake became the focal points of the celebration. The slant trees, those angling toward the sunlight and extending over the lake where no other trees blocked the sunshine, offered ideal photo opportunities for capturing lasting memories. Additionally, the spillway wall served as an ideal spot for precision dives, or perhaps it's more accurately described as comical jumps?

Bill Miller wasn't at the lakeside graduation party. He passed away in 1963, a victim of "black lung disease" attributed to years of inhaling coal dust. During that time, Pennsylvania provided compensation to families after confirming the cause through an autopsy. Medical staff encouraged an autopsy to secure the benefit money. 'You're not cutting up my Bill,' Florence cried… and continued to cry. Consequently, Bill Miller's death certificate attributes his passing to heart attack due to congestive heart failure, and "black lung disease" was not listed as a contributing factor. Despite the much-needed financial assistance, her wishes were honored.

The next year, it was young Bob's turn for war—the Vietnam War. He joined the U.S. Air Force as a Sergeant, often referred to as a Buck Sergeant, holding the rank of a three-striper. During a leave back in the States, he married Barbara Bahrenburg. Whenever he was home, Bob would ask Memmy for the cottage keys, regardless of the season or whether the cottage was open or shut. He and Barb would visit Silver Lake to seek comfort and tranquility before returning to the chaos of war and deployment.

Memmy and her eldest grand-daughter Donna frequently made the trip to the cottage in the 60's after Bill's death. Donna, raised in an urban area, loved the cottage. One day, a girl from across the lake came knocking on the cottage's screen door. She had heard that a girl her age was staying at the

Precise perfection: A flawless launch into the lake from the spillway (Courtesy of Donna Miller Sistek)

Linger Longer, and in that instant, Suzy and Donna formed a fast friendship. Suzy, acting as a mentor, introduced Donna to the ways of the lake. Suzy taught Donna how to fish, clean, and cook the catch of the day, and taught her canoeing. There were also opportunities to ride and brush Suzy's horse Daisy Mae. When the school year was out for the summer and the cottage was opened, Donna eagerly anticipated her time with Suzy and the cottage.

Continuing the legacy with love and memories: Donna and Memmy at the cottage (Courtesy of Gary W. Peck)

It was during this time that Barbara Miller and her husband Jack Webb (veteran of the Korean War), the youngest daughter and son-in-law of the senior Millers, would bring along the youngest grandchildren. I happen to be the eldest among these grandchildren, with my sisters Lisa and Michele following.

As our car transitioned from the macadam road onto the gravel path leading to the cottages, all our senses came alive. The car's engine slowing down and the tires crunching on the gravel signaled our arrival. Stepping out of the car, the gentle rustling of the wind through the hemlock needles welcomed us.

The fragrances were equally enchanting. Towering pine trees filled the air with the delightful aroma of their needles, while the earthy scents from the nearby lake added its unique character to the atmosphere.

Upon exiting the car and turning toward the cottage, we were greeted by the afternoon sun shimmering off the lake's surface, breathtaking.

But there was no time to stand around. We children eagerly raced down the steps, past the pump and outhouse and around the cottage, rushing to catch our first glimpse of the lake. However, before our adventures could truly begin, we made a dash back to the pump house. There, we'd vigorously pull the handle until cold, mineral-rich water gushed forth. Even after letting go of the handle, the water continued to flow, and we'd eagerly cup our hands under the spout, quenching our thirst, whether we were thirsty or not. It was a simple, refreshing ritual that marked the beginning of another memorable visit to Silver Lake.

On September 7, 1972, widowed and amid family-wide financial challenges, Florence sold the cottage using a similar approach to how Bill had acquired it, relying on trusted relationships. While shopping at the Kline Village Farmers Market, she found a buyer in her favorite butcher.

After our multi-state start to married life, Kathy and I settled in the D.C. suburbs to raise our children near our families. On a trip to Harrisburg in 1988, I turned to her and said, "Let me show you where I spent my summers as a child." It didn't take us long to locate the realtor's lockbox hanging on the Linger Longer's doorknob – a clear sign that the cottage was listed for sale.

The imminent sale was prompted by the installation of public sewers to replace outhouses. However, given the extensive rot and insect damage, retrofitting the half-century plus summer cottage with indoor plumbing was impractical. The most reasonable course of action was a complete teardown and rebuild. So, on May 1, 1989, seventeen years after Florence sold it, we bought the cottage back into the family to launch its next version.

Before commencing the teardown, we extended an invitation to the older generations to pay one last visit – and they were delighted. The new Linger Longer continues to serve as a family gathering place. It isn't about opulence; it is about the simple joys of family, shared laughter, and creating enduring memories for all who come together here.

Nostalgia and laughter as Michael Torchia and Donna Miller Sistek revisit their youthful days at Silver Lake (Authors' Photograph)

The legacy of the lakeside anniversary endures as descendants gather 60 years later for a joyful family reunion, celebrating their enduring bond. In the center of the photo stand Steve, Bob, Bob's wife Barb, and Donna (Authors' Photograph)

SILVER LAKE'S SILVER-BLUE CLAY

Hidden Beneath the Soil: Bentonite Clay Unearthed
(Authors' Photograph)

SILVER LAKE'S SILVER-BLUE CLAY

The origin of the name "Silver Lake" is a mystery with various "interpretations." According to one belief, the name harkens back to the lake's exceptional historical water clarity, with the tale that a silver coin could be dropped into the lake and remain visible at the lake's bottom. Yet, others claim the lake's shimmering silver color on clear moonlit nights is the source of the name. Another theory suggests a possible connection between the name and the presence of silverish-blue clay deposits believed to have been discovered in the lakebed during the excavation. Meanwhile, an alternate viewpoint speculates that the name may have arisen from the use of blue clay to seal leaks at the lake's dam or spillway.

Given its crucial role as a source of energy, the millers could not afford to lose water and, by extension, the energy required to power the mill due to leaks. To ensure water preservation, measures were taken, including lining ponds or sealing leaks with sheets of clay.

In the accompanying photo, a Silver Lake resident displays a ball of Bentonite clay she unearthed while working in her garden.[84] During dam and seawall repairs, when the lake is drawn down, some residents seize the opportunity to harvest the nutrient-rich silt from the lake's bottom. It is plausible that in the past, during such a harvesting episode, the ball of clay was brought to the surface and inadvertently ended up in a flower bed.

To gain further insights into the potential connection between the clay and the lake's name, we investigated the nature of the clay itself. This particular type of clay is known as Bentonite, and it was likely brought in to line the lake. However, it's important to note that this Bentonite clay isn't naturally present beneath Silver Lake. Instead, it was probably sourced from a nearby location, potentially from Franklin or Lycoming counties, but not directly on-site.[85,86]

Bentonite serves as a stable, impermeable layer beneath the water, preventing drainage. The deposits of Bentonite found in the much older Chambersburg Formation located two counties away, can be traced back to the Ordovician period. Bentonite is a clay known for its high shrink-swell ratio. It can be mixed with existing soils and compacted in layers. When wet, Bentonite swells significantly, creating a compacted clay soil layer that aids in retaining water within the pond. It is possible that Bentonite was utilized in an attempt to address leak issues, especially near the spillway, as Silver Lake experienced problems with leakage in that specific area.

In the course of researching the William G. Stonesifer family, a Stonesifer genealogy website provided the initial insights into William G. Stonesifer, including his occupation as a sawyer and details about his immediate family. Within this digital archive, a diary authored by Frank J. Penington, a relative of Stonesifer, emerged, titled, "Journal of Frank J. Penington." This diary, dating back to 1862 when Frank was a 13-year-old boy, shed light on the leisure activities of young individuals from that era, particularly Frank Penington's passion for fishing and swimming in a millpond known as "Silver Lake."

Interestingly, while some of Frank Penington's Stonesifer ancestors had settled in the nearby town of Lewisberry, it was evident that his reference was not to the Silver Lake in Lewisberry but rather to a Silver Lake in Middletown, Delaware. The fact that both of these mill ponds were named "Silver Lake" and were located in close proximity to Stonesifer family members is indeed a remarkable coincidence.[87]

The utilization of sheets or pads made from this clay to line specific areas of lakebed could potentially provide an explanation for the name "Silver Lake," as the lake might have had a silver-like appearance, especially when reflecting sunlight. Considering the importance of maintaining substantial water reservoirs to power mills in the 1700s and 1800s, it is reasonable to speculate that Bentonite was commonly used in mill ponds of that era. This use of Bentonite could have contributed to the name "Silver Lake" being used for both the Fairview Township, Pennsylvania, and Middletown, Delaware mill ponds.

In truth, there are numerous lakes named Silver Lake scattered across the United States. This name is widespread among lakes in various regions, resulting in differing counts. Typically, these lakes derive their name from the shimmering appearance of their waters. The term Silver Lake is quite popular, and each of these lakes boasts distinct features. For instance, Michigan lays claim to nine inland lakes named Silver Lake[88], while Pennsylvania hosts Silver Lakes in Susquehanna County fed by Silver Creek (near Quaker Lake), Bucks County (originating as another man-made mill pond in 1687), and York County.

The origin of the name "Silver Lake" remains uncertain, lending an element of entertainment to its speculation. This allows individuals to formulate their own theories regarding its origins, creating a harmless and enjoyable guessing game about what is indeed a relatively trivial matter.

Beneath the Surface: Underwater Fishing Prowess:
Belted Kingfisher (Courtesy of Ken Boyer)

THE SPILLWAY

Nature's Power Unleashed: Torrents Rush Through the Narrow Spillway
Channel (Courtesy of Lee Margot)

THE SPILLWAY

The Silver Lake watershed area has changed substantially over its 250-year history. Agricultural land has in many places given way to residential housing, and the presence of gutters, drains, roads, and culverts accelerates the movement of stormwater towards Silver Lake. This acceleration leads to a more rapid increase in the pool of water than was seen when the land was exclusively farmland and forests. Consequently, the lake's water level rises more swiftly. In the absence of effective management of this elevation, there is a potential risk of over-topping, and eventual breach of the dam. This would cause significant damage. An example of such a circumstance occurred during Hurricane Ida in September 2021, when locally heavy rainfall resulted in the brief over-topping of the 250 year old earthen dam.

In the event of a breach of the Silver Lake earthen dam, the water would not surge out like the torrent of the Johnstown Flood; instead, it would release a wall of water and mud a few inches high for hours as the reservoir gradually drained from the lake. However, it's crucial to recognize that swiftly moving water even just a few inches high can sweep away a car or knock a person off their feet. It's this potential danger that earned Silver Lake the classification of a High-Hazard Dam (Size Category C Impoundment Storage less than 1,000 (Acre Feet), Hazard Potential 2 – Population at Risk, a Loss of a Few Lives) in 2013 by the Pennsylvania Department of Environmental Protection (PA-DEP).

The spillway system was originally designated in the SLCA by-laws to fall under the jurisdiction of the SLCA Dams and Streams Committee, responsible for all matters related to the lake's dams and streams. It is situated at the northern end of Silver Lake and is engineered to manage excess water. Unlike the earthen dam, which remains substantially unchanged over the centuries, the spillway has seen some modern modifications.

The spillway fulfills three primary functions: regulating the water level of the reservoir, guiding water safely downstream, and reducing the velocity of the water flow before it enters natural channels. In the photograph depicting the "new" spillway constructed in the early 1960s below, the spillway's design becomes apparent.[89]

Water streams over the crest of the structure, forming a cascading flow down the concrete "S" shape on the downstream side, efficiently dispersing energy during this process. The spillway has undergone expansion to around 80 feet in width, creating a more extensive area for water overflow when a rapid release is needed. Furthermore, as part of the 1960's construction project, trees and their root balls were extracted from the earthy section of

Optimized Design: Enhancing Energy
Dissipation in the Spillway

the former spillway to diminish underground pathways for seepage. The decaying roots were contributing to both the escalation in seepage velocity and volume.

In addition to aiding in water level regulation, gates equipped with stoplogs can release water downstream. Beyond the spillway, walls made of brownstone and concrete confine the water as it continues its journey towards natural channels. It passes beneath Siddonsburg Road and enters a small pond once known locally as "Sticks Pond." From this point, the water follows its course, making its way to Bennett Run.

Before the 1960s, the "old" spillway appears to have taken the form of a narrow straight drop design. Believed to have been constructed c. 1930, it consisted of a wall, or weir, positioned with its downstream face in a vertical orientation. When the water level in the reservoir exceeded the standard pool level, the excess water would cascade freely from the crest of the weir. The constriction of the water's course as it entered the narrow brownstone and concrete channel caused the water to flow swiftly and with great force.

During periods of low water levels, the weir wall could serve a dual purpose as a narrow walkway, allowing access to the opposite side of the spillway. Excess water was released during high-water periods by passing over the weir wall. Observed from above, one saw a smooth, glass-like expanse of water cascading off the wall, then crashing below. The water took on the illusion of an infinity pool—crystal clear, mesmerizing, and, to an eight-year-old boy in 1951, deceptively inviting.

Beneath the crashing water, however, lies significant danger for anyone who might accidentally fall in. For a drowning victim caught beneath a waterfall, survival hinges on overcoming powerful hydrological forces. These include the sheer force and substantial volume of water plummeting from the top which can take an object to the bottom of the stream, the turbulent flow resulting from the cascading water, and the occurrence of an entrapment zone that creates a turbulent and aerated environment, diminishing buoyancy and generating a forceful recirculating current that can trap and hold a victim underwater for hours.

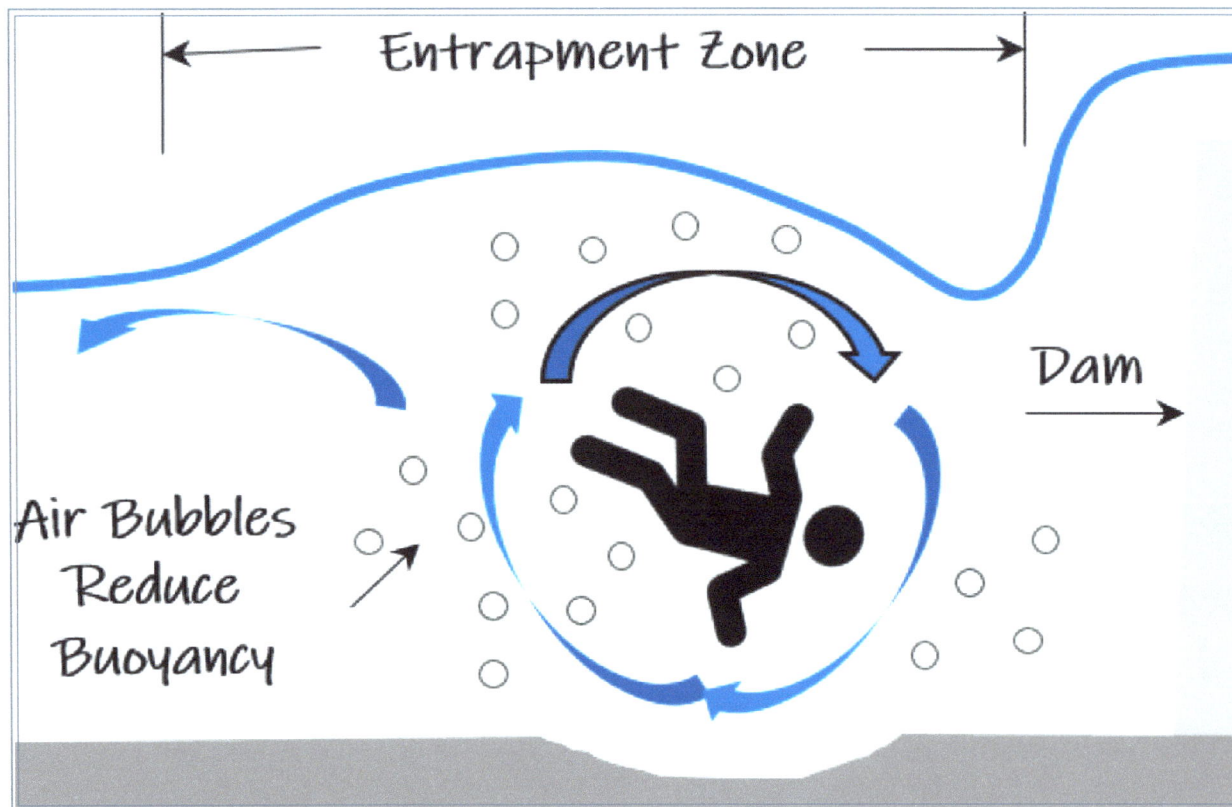

Recirculating currents below the dam can trap and drown victims
(Authors' illustration)

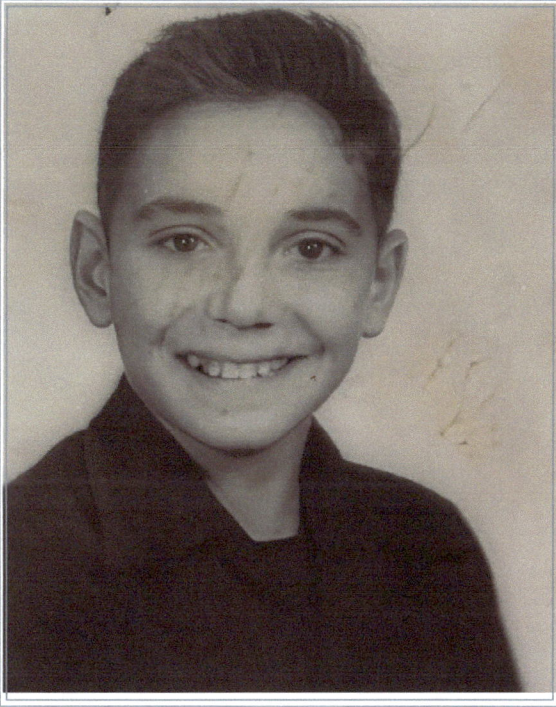

The Smile of Survival: Andy Torchia's Harrowing Experience (Courtesy of H. Andrew Torchia, Jr.)

As eight-year-old Andy Torchia took one step, and then another across the overflowing spillway, his feet were suddenly swept from beneath him by the rushing water. He was carried over the side into the perilous and turbulent current below. In an instant, he recognized the danger and realized that his life was in jeopardy. His mind screamed with prayer, pleading for help to escape and find safety.

In Andy's own words, "The water was rushing over the entire dam walkway (not just through the spillway). Like a stupid kid, I started walking through the water on the wide concrete walkway and was swept over and under the water below. I was underwater holding my breath. I started praying and felt a hand that guided me to the wall with the triangular stones on top. I grabbed a stone and somehow pulled myself out of the rushing water to safety. A moment in time that I will never forget."[90]

Guided by his "Angel buddies" who helped him reach the wall, along with the combined strength of an eight-year-old boy and his lightweight frame, Andy managed to pull himself out of the water. The triangular stone Andy mentioned was one of the pointed coping stones on the red/brownstone walls. Serving as a gripping point to rescue a young drowning victim is yet another role of these pointed coping stones.

Red-tailed Hawk (Courtesy of Ken Boyer)

TRAINING
YOUNG
PEOPLE

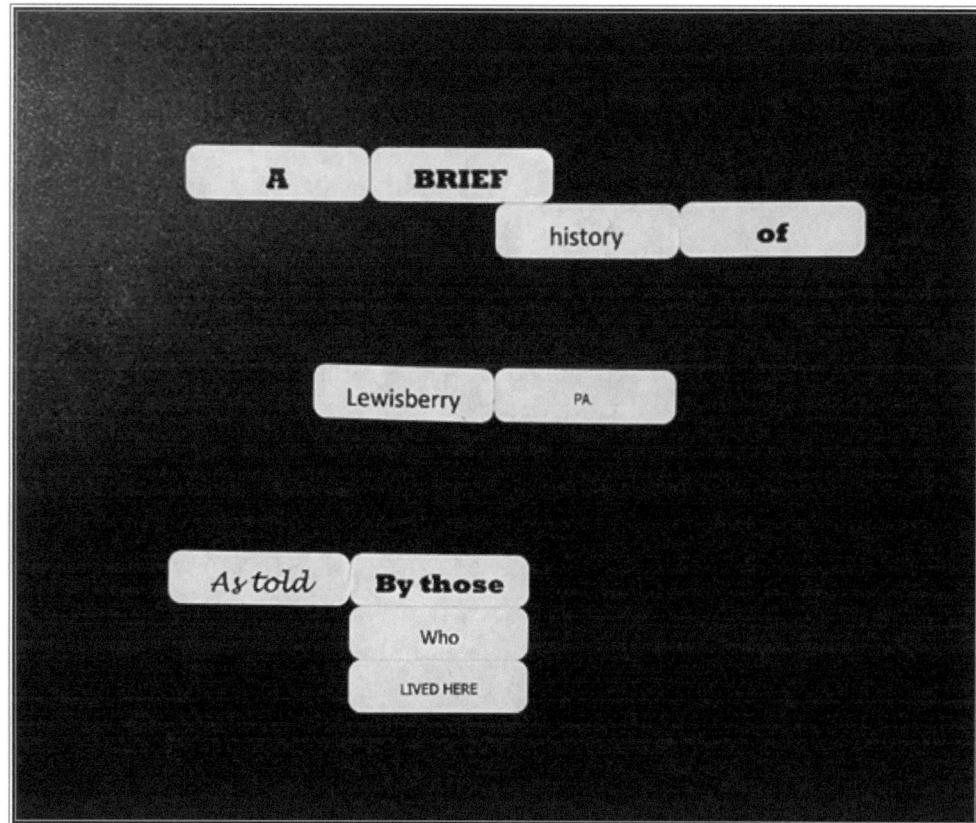

Mt. Zion Elementary School's Sixth Grade Pupils' "A Brief History of Lewisberry PA. as Told by Those Who Live Here."

TRAINING YOUNG PEOPLE

In 1955, the South Point Schoolhouse was decommissioned and sold. This resulted in the reassignment of its students to neighboring schools equipped with modern amenities like flush toilets. In the academic year of 1963 to 1964, Donald Snelbaker, then teacher at Mt. Zion Elementary School, Fairview Township, Pennsylvania, challenged his 6th grade class with this question: "What do we know about our own area?" The students' response took the form of a booklet, which has now become a piece of history. Their intention was "to present what we found, so that perhaps more vestiges of the past can be preserved for the future." The booklet, well documented, comprises letters, newspaper articles, photographs, and interviews with local oldsters born in the mid-1800s recorded on the occasion of the United States Sesquicentennial celebrations.[91]

The topics are diverse, spanning from the establishment of the town of Lewisberry and its layout (inclusive of a detailed house-by-house description), to discussions of local industries and occupations, Civil War veterans, early postmasters, and recollections of W. Scott Hammond during his youth. Hammond, a Lewisberry businessman, achieved recognition for his role in introducing mechanization to his father's window sash company. In a 1924 interview, he shared boyhood memories from 1856 to 1863. Interestingly, in sharing his boyhood memories, he references the lake but never by its name, 'Silver Lake'.[92]

"The first thing a little boy did", Mr. Hammond says, "was to learn to fish with a pin hook in Bennett Run at the edge of the town. Then, when he got money enough and was old enough to get a real fish hook, he went to the dam just a little beyond town and fished with the real grown-up men and big boys. He used any kind of fishing pole; however, a real cane fishing rod was far beyond the reach of any boy, and only a few of the men possessed such a wonderful outfit in those days. The first fish we caught were roaches," said Mr. Hammond, "and once in a while a sun fish, and then perhaps a cat fish, but it was a big event in the neighborhood when any of us boys caught a pike. Everybody quit fishing then for that day, and we all crowded around the hero, escorted him in triumph through the village, and almost fought to get next to him, and perhaps be given a 'turn' at carrying the big fish."

Bennett Run was where the Lewisberry borough boys first learned to swim. In a deep hole, about three feet deep and twenty feet long, they started by swimming downstream in a simple manner. Then, they would exit the water, run back to the top of the swimming hole, and repeat the process.

> *After we could swim for a little bit, we graduated to that part of the dam considered a special place for small boys. By and by, we could venture out farther on a rail, and then, when the whole gang could get on a big log about seventy-five feet long, the fun really began. That log seemed to be a part of the dam for years. We didn't know how it got there, but we surely made use of it since it was there.*

Hammond and his group of friends considered the entire outdoors their playground, assigning proper names to geographical features like Church Hill and Reiff's Mountain. However, it is curious that there is no mention of the name "Silver Lake" in their accounts, even though his boyhood activities often brought them to the lake's edge for fishing and involved swimming in the lake itself. In subsequent recollections, Hammond describes gathering alder roots beneath the big breast of the dam - built in the late 1700s and the only dam near town—without connecting it to Silver Lake. Considering the lack of Silver Lake references in recollections from the 1860s, its omission from October 1883 Cline survey of the lake and surroundings, and the postmark date of the Silver Lake postcard on September 18, 1913, it's reasonable to deduce that Silver Lake received its name between 1883 and 1913.

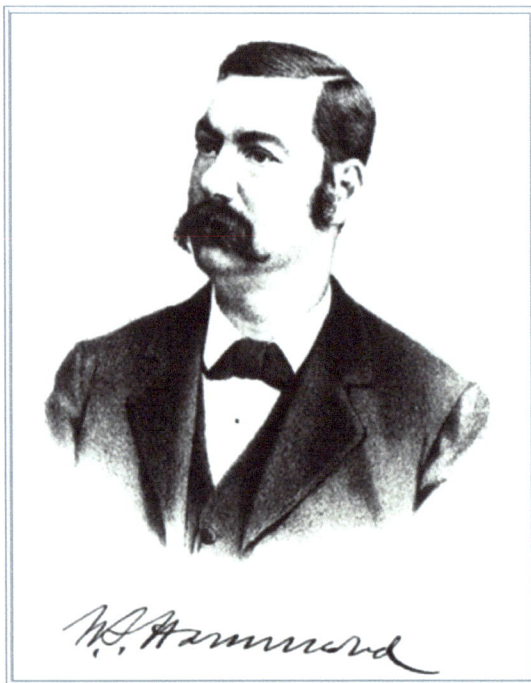

Memories of Boyhood in Lewisberry: W. Scott Hammond's Recollections

In March 1865, W. Scott Hammond's boyhood years came to an end as he enlisted as a Private in Company I, 192nd Pennsylvania Volunteers during the American Civil War.[93] Later, he married Miss Jeannette Starr, and together they raised three children.[94] Subsequently, he assumed the responsibility for his father, Hervey Hammond's business, which was centered around the patented Hammond window sash spring—a product of historical significance. Notably, in 1838, President Martin Van Buren had Hammond springs installed in all the windows of the White House. W. Scott Hammond lived to age 85.[95,96]

Donald Eugene Snelbaker lived his passion for "training young people," as the teaching profession is referred to in "A Brief History of Lewisberry, PA as Told by Those Who Lived Here." Snelbaker, initially a teacher and later a principal, went on to serve as a School Administrator for the West Shore School District in New Cumberland, Pennsylvania.[97] Toward the end of his life, at age 92, and still in possession of the 6th grader's assignment, he requested his favorite barber, a steward of history herself, to safeguard the document. She has since provided it to the authors, thus becoming the next link in the chain of provenance.[98] We subsequently entrusted it to the York County History Center in York, Pennsylvania, thereby fulfilling the students' request to ensure that the remnants and traces of the area's historical and cultural elements from the past are preserved for the benefit of future generations.[99]

Donald E. Snelbaker, 1948 York College

SOUTH POINT SCHOOLHOUSE REMEMBRANCES

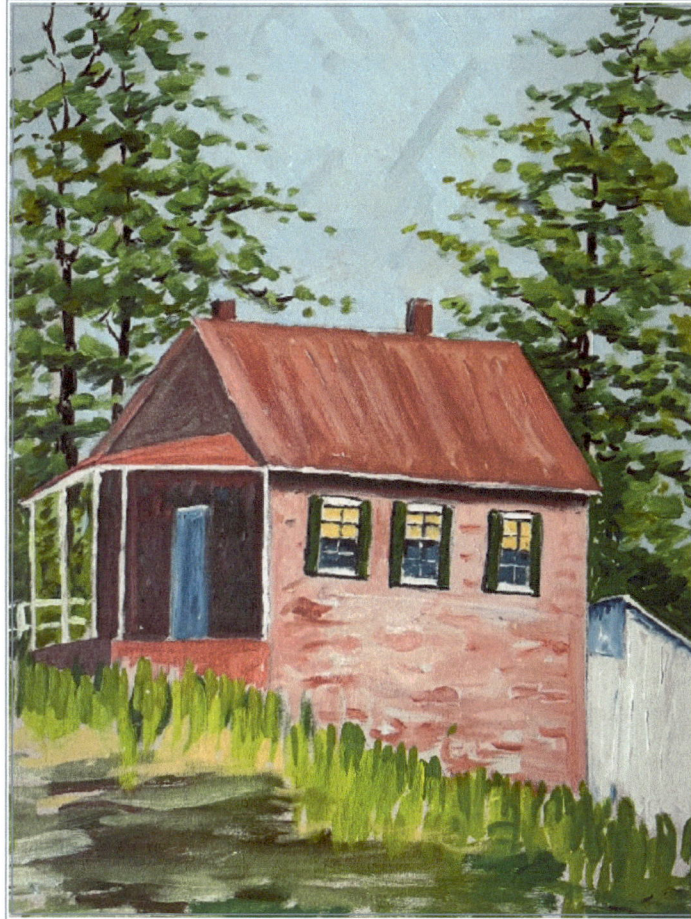

Vibrant Memories: The South Point Schoolhouse in
Bold Hues (Courtesy of H. Andrew Torchia, Jr.)

SOUTH POINT SCHOOLHOUSE REMEMBRANCES

Andy Torchia cherishes the memories of his days at the one-room red stone South Point Schoolhouse. He reminisces, "No child was ever left behind. Whenever a student grappled with a lesson, Mrs. Effie Snyder would pair them with an older classmate for personalized assistance. This arrangement not only aided the younger student by providing individual attention but also benefited the older student, who reinforced their own learning by teaching the concept to someone else." [100]

Andy recalls how the indomitable Mrs. Snyder held sway over a classroom brimming with 60 eager students, a testament to her unwavering command of the learning environment. He recalls the simple ritual of 'call whistle' at the close of recess as symbolizing the harmony of those days. Mrs. Snyder, with no need for a shrill whistle, would simply turn from her desk and address the students closest to the doorway in a gentle voice, uttering the words, "Call 'whistle'." That child would call it outside, and the word would ripple through the group like a shared secret: "whistle." With this, the class seamlessly transitioned back to the serious business of education for another half-day of "training young people." Every detail of the schoolhouse, even down to the two side-by-side outhouses used by the 60 children, is etched in Andy's memory.

Andy recalls his disappointment when his family moved, and he had to leave the school in 6th grade. He says he was so far ahead of his peers academically that he was totally bored in his new school, and became, in his words, a borderline juvenile delinquent. Louise Earnest, the wife of Andy's father's law partner, was well acquainted with the family's affection for the schoolhouse. She lovingly crafted a painted rendition of the schoolhouse as a gift to the Torchia family. The image, displayed on the previous page, radiates vibrant red hues, perhaps a shade too intense. Nonetheless, it remains a cherished relic, harkening back to Andy's youth, and graces the walls of his home to this day.

1949 South Point School Class Photo: Andy Torcia
second row, fifth from the left, Mrs. Effie Snyder
center rear (Courtesy of Barbara Forgas)

However, not everyone held every moment at the South Point Schoolhouse in the same high regard. Barbara Gross Forgas is the daughter of Lester H. and Gladys Gross. She resided in the family's combined general store and house.

Barbara distinctly recalls her experience in those early school days. Barbara was not a fan of school! The town children walked as a group the 5-10 minutes outside Lewisberry borough to the schoolhouse. They passed a young grove of pine trees between town and the school. Six-year-old Barbara made a deliberate choice to linger at the back of the group. She would skillfully slip into the pine trees, creating for herself a neat little outdoor space where she could discreetly watch the final students enter the schoolhouse. With the door closing behind them, ensnaring them in yet another structured day of learning, Barbara's day remained unencumbered. In her concealed retreat, away from the busy classroom, she relished her precious freedom.[101]

She paid close attention to lunch breaks and dismissal, ensuring that she was the first one to reach home for her meal when school let out for the lunch hour. Then, she would skillfully repeat her act on the way back to school. This routine continued for about a week until Mrs. Snyder decided to pay a visit to the Gross family to check on young Barbara, as she had noticed her absence from school for the entire week. This came as a surprise to her parents! Sadly for Barbara, this scheme came to an end.

It didn't take Barbara long to discover that Mrs. Snyder had what would be called today a 'time-out chair,' and she quickly learned how to place herself in it intentionally. This chair held a certain appeal for Barbara, as it was situated between the piano and the southwest corner window. Seated in the 'time-out chair' with the upright piano blocking Mrs. Snyder's and the rest of the class's view, Barbara once again found solace in entertaining herself by observing the events of the outside world.

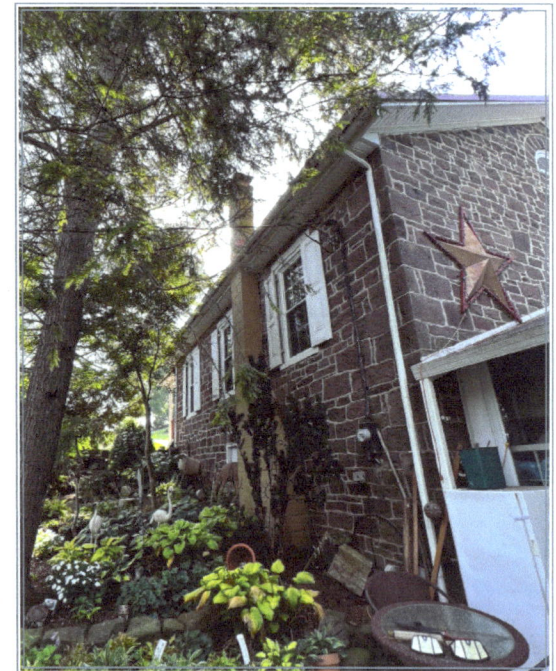

Window, Top Right: The Time-Out Corner's Secret - A Special Connection with the World (Authors' Photograph)

Parents queued up in their cars at the end of the school day to pick up their children, as Barbara recalls. This wasn't about spoiling the children; rather, it was a means for parents to prevent their children from dawdling on their way home and to ensure that they could promptly attend to their chores.

The Grosses were a thrifty family, often using products that were aging on the grocery store shelves as dinner ingredients. "My mother would save the paper the butter came in, use it to wrap margarine, place it on our kitchen table, and try to convince us we were eating butter," Barbara recalls. "Another example," she continues, "I could never get used to the smell of old meat being cooked and served for dinner." Pasteboard boxes - a stiff, firm board made of sheets of paper pasted together - were sturdy and large enough to function as cribs for Barbara's twin brothers, delivered by Old Doc H.C. Hetrick's son, Dr. Eugene Hetrick, also of Lewisberry.

The Gross family's thriftiness eventually paid off, first allowing them to purchase a property on Silver Lake, as other town dwellers had done. Second, it made it possible to fulfill Gladys Gross's dream of building a stately manor house graced with majestic white columns, radiating an air of grandeur and classical elegance. This new manor was constructed across the street from their old house. Additionally, they built the new Gross' general store adjacent to their home, and it was aptly named the 'Manor-ette' in homage to the grandeur of the manor house.

Barbara's time as a student at South Point Schoolhouse came to a close in 1954, after the institution that had served as an educational haven for local youth for 157 years was decommissioned.

Over the years, she completed her education, married David Forgas, raised a family, and ventured into running a landscaping business. At times, she had a cottage on Silver Lake. Her journey came full circle when she purchased the South Point Schoolhouse with the intention of opening "Bonsai at South Point Schoolhouse." Barbara encountered opposition from some local residents who sought to block her from opening her business, citing zoning regulations. As scrappy as ever, she defended her position, arguing that the cultivation, harvesting,

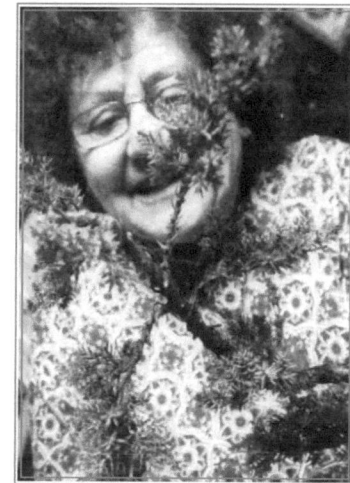

Bonsai Beauty: The Art of Careful Trimming
Kuehnel, P. (Photographer). (13 September 2011). "The Zen Growth" - Photo of Barbara Forgas. p.7. The Daily News, Lebanon, Pennsylvania

and sale of bonsai constituted a form of farming—a perspective that found favor with local officials, and her business was approved. Trees, with their tranquil aura, continue to offer serenity to both Barbara and her customers, making it an ideal enterprise for retirement.[102]

It's a familiar narrative, where a student defies expectations, overcoming obstacles to thrive and forge their unique path to success. The journey from being underestimated to achieving while staying true to oneself is the natural order of things. Today, only two pine trees stand as a reminder of the once welcoming grove of trees that provided refuge to young Barbara.

The 1953 South Point School class photo below features Barbara Gross in the first row second from the right. In the background you will find the diminutive Mrs. Effie Snyder.

1953 Class Photo: Barbara Gross Forgas at South Point School (Courtesy of Barbara Forgas)

MORE FIGURES IN SILVER LAKE'S STORY

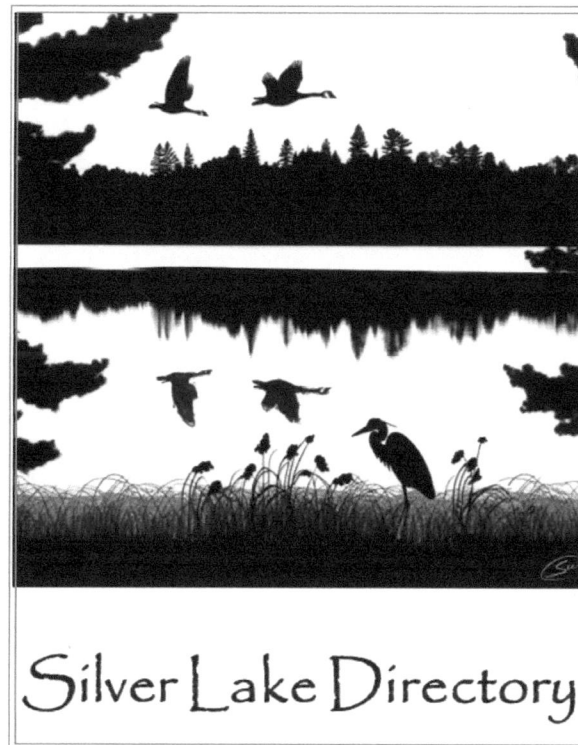

Silver Lake Directory

Pre-privacy era: Circa 1990 directory cover, recreated
from memory, recalling a time when names,
addresses, and phone numbers were openly shared
(Authors' illustration)

MORE FIGURES IN
SILVER LAKE'S STORY

Ruth Stonesifer, a genealogist, mother, and activist, significantly aided the authors' research by providing an initial breakthrough with her Delaware Diamonds Genealogy website, which detailed the ancestry of William Grant Stonesifer. Ruth Stonesifer's son, Kristofor "Kris" Stonesifer, lost his life in action in Pakistan during the October 2001 Enduring Freedom campaign. In honor of Kris, Ruth actively pursued legislative measures, successfully advocating for a bill in the Pennsylvania legislature to establish specialized license plates for Gold Star Families, orchestrating the display of Hometown Heroes banners, and serving as the 2009-2010 National President of the American Gold Star Mothers organization.[103]

Lewis Cline, one of ten children, grew up as a farmer and later became a teacher. He took over his father's mill (Andrew Cline) upon his passing and ran it independently. In 1871, he married Elmira Mordorf, and they had three children: Clara, Rosaline, and Edith. Lewis, who served in the Civil War with company K, 130th Pennsylvania Volunteer infantry, was wounded at Antietam, leading to a lifelong disability. A proud member of Lincoln's party, his service and sacrifice marked his contributions.[104] Notably, during his ownership of the grist mill and the surrounding land, Silver Lake received its name.

Edith Cline, Lewis Cline's daughter, served as the Lewisberry correspondent for The Gazette and Daily, York Pennsylvania, for over three decades.[105] Throughout this period, she meticulously chronicled the history of Lewisberry, offering detailed descriptions of residents and businesses, house by house. Her writings remain a valuable contribution to our current understanding of both Lewisberry and Silver Lake. Edith Cline played a significant role in preserving her family's legacy as mill operators and championing her father's vision of a Silver Lake resort. She had a close friendship with William G. and Mary A. Stonesifer. During their golden wedding anniversary celebration, where Mary A. Stonesifer received a bouquet of 50 beautiful, large red roses, Miss Edith Cline was presented with one of those beautiful roses.[106]

Ivan C. Frey, the founder of the Spring Garden Brick company and later the President of the York Colonial Brick Company (1939), was an early investor in Silver Lake properties. He was the second individual to purchase a lot from William G. Stonesifer. The Frey family actively participated in the operational affairs of the lake, notably becoming one of the larger shareholders of the Silver Lake Improvement Company and serving as President. The Frey's also maintained social ties with the Cline family, as documented in newspapers of the time.[107]

In 1948, at the age of 63, Ivan C. Frey ended his life with a self-inflicted gunshot wound. Yet, drawing a connection between his suicide and SLIC's perceived failure is disputable, challenging the local lore. SLIC had successfully sold the last unsold lots by this time, setting the stage for the successor nonprofit association, Silver Lake Community Association. Frey, at the time of his passing, was affluent, leaving an estate worth $135,600, equivalent to $1.7 million in 2023.[108] Newspaper reports state that Frey had suffered from poor health for a year prior to his death.[109] This could imply that a terminally ill individual might have chosen the timing and manner of their passing.

Otis H. Barnes played vital roles in selling lots owned by William G. Stonesifer and later the Silver Lake Improvement Company. First, as a Justice of the Peace in Rossville, York County, Pennsylvania, he became a trusted authority for verifying and validating deeds, ensuring their legality and proper recording. Secondly, despite losing two fingers in a gas-powered mixing machine accident at his brother's ice cream shop, with treatment from Dr. H. Bruce Hetrick,[110] Otis Barnes pursued a career as a surveyor and draftsman. He meticulously surveyed and drafted the vision outlined by William G. Stonesifer for the development of the area surrounding Silver Lake. Sadly, despite a diligent search by county staff, only the Marie Avenue subdivision plans were found in the York County Archives.

Dr. H. Bruce Hetrick, a lifelong resident of Warrington Township, was the son of Dr. and Mrs. A.C. Hetrick and the grandson of Dr. and Mrs. Joseph Hayward. For six decades, he was actively engaged in the practice of medicine, including tending to the injury of Otis Barnes in 1913, upholding a tradition of family physicians that originated when his grandfather opened an office in 1801. This legacy was carried forward by Dr. Henry B. Hoff of Wellsville and Dr. Homer C. Hetrick of Lewisberry, both nephews of Dr. H.B. Hetrick.[111]

Dr. Homer C. Hetrick (Old Doc), husband of Harriet Beecher Stowe Stonesifer Hetrick and a resident of Lewisberry, obtained his medical degree in 1906, a century after his great-grandfather established a practice in Rossville. During his 44 years of rural medical practice, he earned a reputation for never turning down a patient's call or pressing for payments.[112] Dr. Hetrick acquired a lot on Silver Lake's West Street, originally purchased by his father Mr. Gurney H. Hetrick, a merchant who notably was not a doctor, and was one of the initial buyers of Stonesifer lots in July 1927.[113] At Dr. H. C. Hetrick's funeral services in 1952, more than 600 people attended, reflecting sentiments such as "We'll never have another doctor like him." The subsequent year, over 800 individuals gathered for a service honoring Dr. H.C. Hetrick, leading to the installation of a memorial bronze plaque.[114] The inscription on the plaque reads:

Dedicated to the memory of Dr. Homer C. Hetrick, M. D. who served as our beloved country doctor (with over 6,000 babies delivered), 1908 to 1952. His life of tireless efforts and faithful devotion to his practice will be forever a source of living inspiration to the community he loved and served so well.[115]

A memorial plaque for Dr. Homer C. Hetrick, M.D.
at a Lewisberry historical marker.

Dr. G. Eugene "Gene" "Doc" Hetrick, Dr. H.C. Hetrick's son, an Army veteran of World War II where he served as a doctor in a medical unit following the Normandy invasion, returned and established part of his practice in Lewisberry, dedicating most of his time to treating returning World War II soldiers at the Harrisburg Veterans Administration hospital. In 1956, he pursued an advanced medical degree in psychiatry to enhance his ability to work at the Veterans Administration.[116] The Hetrick doctors' dedication to their rural patients was evident once again by Dr. Eugene Hetrick's practice of making house calls, including providing medical care to the Torchia children at their residence for a nominal fee of $1, and assisting in the delivery of Barbara Gross Forgas' twin brothers."[117]

Harry F. Peck, the husband of Shirley R. Miller and son-in-law of Bill and Florence Miller, served in the U.S. Navy during World War II as an Electricians Mate 2nd class and kept a diary. He was aboard the LCTA-2037, which was part of the 6th wave at Omaha Beach during the amphibious assault of Operation Overlord.[118] The LCTA-2037 was a British craft that had been "reverse lend-leased" back to the US for the Normandy invasion. These vessels did not beach; their mission was to provide close gunfire support.[119] A German artillery shell struck his landing craft on its return to the convoy, rendering it inoperable. Despite efforts to retrieve it, the craft remained stranded off the shore, exposed to continuous fire from German fortifications on the hills above the beach. It could not be towed due to the movement of other vessels, which were following orders to ferry soldiers to and from the beach. Following the war, Harry Peck frequently visited the 'Linger Longer' cottage on Silver Lake, seeking peace and tranquility punctuated by occasional raucous family gatherings. There were no entries in his diary after June 5th, 1944.

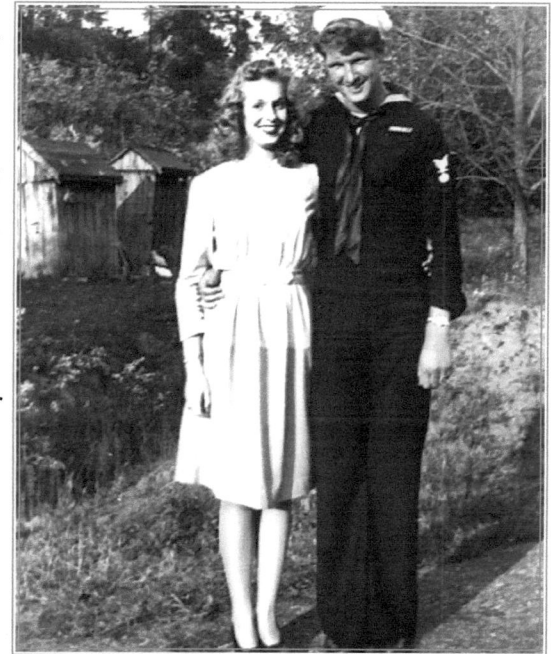

Harry F. Peck in military uniform with his wife, Shirley R. Miller Peck (Courtesy of Gary W. Peck)

Robert "Bobbie" Vernon Stonesifer, Sr. Son of Guy and Mabel Stonesifer, grandson of William G. and Mary A. Stonesifer, and husband of Janice Good Stonesifer. Guy Stonesifer's sudden death, according to the Medical Examiner, was attributed to acute nephritis, also known as kidney failure. And while some young married couples are not prepared for the sudden loss of a spouse – youthful invincibility, overreliance on youthful good health – Mabel was better prepared than others. Mabel Heiges Stonesifer had a personal understanding of the challenges and hardships that come with growing up without a father, just as Bobbie would. Her father, John Heiges, tragically lost his life in a mining accident when she was only four-years-old.[120] Her own mother's experience when she suddenly became a widow with young children gave Mabel insight, at 23 years of age, into her own future.

Sgt. Robert V. Stonesifer U.S. Army
(Courtesy of Jillian Stonesifer Teasley)

Bobbie was raised by his mother and caring paternal aunts. Newspaper articles continued to refer to him as "Bobbie" as he regularly visited his extended Stonesifer family at Silver Lake. (Mabel relocated after Guy's passing so their bungalow was available to the next miller, Levi Shaffer.)

When old enough, Bobbie would attend the Milton Hershey School, an institution for fatherless boys, where he would receive an education encompassing academics, vocational training – he chose carpentry, and a foundation in faith.[121] Mabel would take the bus on weekends from Lancaster, and then later Mechanicsburg to Hershey to spend time with her son. She instilled in him, and later in his children, the art of letter writing, emphasizing the profound sharing of emotions and life experiences. Mabel remarried when Bobbie finished school, and the new family relocated to Bridgeton, New Jersey.

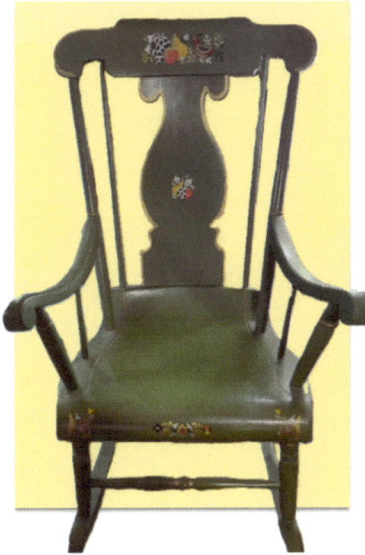

Robert's meticulous restoration work: Aunt Ora Stonesifer's rocking chair shines in beautiful Jamestown Green. (Authors' illustration using photo provided by Jillian Stonesifer Teasley)

with Robert William Miller. If they ever met, it's unlikely that they discussed Silver Lake, as Bobbie Stonesifer had been removed from his lake experience for several years, and Robert Miller had yet to visit the "Linger Longer" cottage his father purchased in July 1945.

Upon completing his service, he returned to New Jersey. There, Bobbie met his future wife, Janice Good, on a blind date arranged by their respective mothers. They married in 1951, and he pursued a career as a carpenter and cabinet maker, even constructing several family homes during their 63 years of marriage.[122] Together they raised two children, and upon retirement relocated to Florida near their eldest.[123]

Despite growing up without a father, Bobbie was well-cared for. When individuals choose a life partner, they go through a phase of self-reflection and consider what qualities they desire in a long-term companion. In Mabel, Guy chose a strong and resilient woman as his wife; he chose wisely.

Bobbie, now going by the nickname 'Stoney,' a shortened form of his family name, served in the U.S. Army as a Sergeant, stationed in post-war Germany, where his carpentry training uniquely qualified him to support reconstruction. He was particularly well-suited for the task of rebuilding Germany's infrastructure. It was during this time that he coincidentally served in country

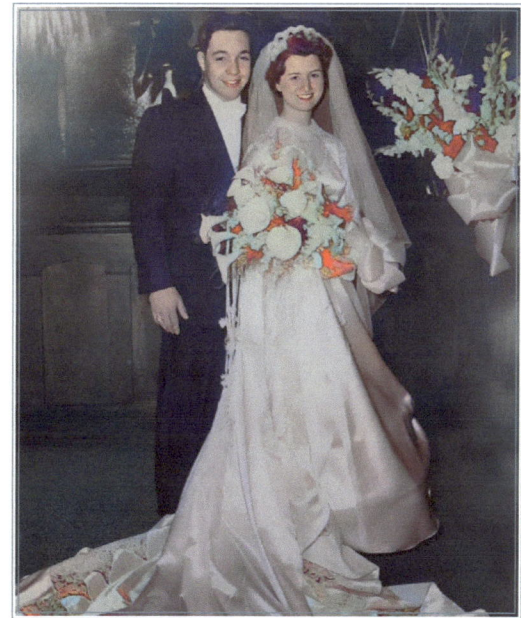

From Blind Date to Soulmates: Janice and Robert's 61-Year Love Affair (Courtesy of Jillian Stonesifer Teasley)

ACKNOWLEDGEMENTS

As the sun sets, one Pennsylvania girl (Texas shirt notwithstanding) looks back with gratitude. This acknowledgment is a humble thank-you to all who contributed to this story

ACKNOWLEDGMENTS

A work like this is impossible without the help and encouragement of many people. This is a modest effort to acknowledge and thank those who shared their time, talent, and treasure to bring this story alive.

We offer heartfelt thanks and appreciation to Andy, Kathy, Michael, and Marge Torchia, who shared their memories of growing up on "Torchia Hill," the South Point Schoohouse, precious family photographs and not least of all their time and friendship.

To Lee Margot who spent hours sharing her family's history and memories, welcomed us into her Log Haven, and gifted us with photographs and documents.

Barbara Forgas, you are a treasure! The afternoon learning about the South Point Schoolhouse, your personal stories and your amazing collection of photographs through the years were a memorable part of our journey.

To the Stonesifer family, especially Bob Jr. and Jillian, for taking the time to unearth and share your family photographs, and for sharing 'the rest of the story' about Mabel and Bob Sr.

And last but not least, our Miller clan, to Bob and Steve Miller, Donna Sistek and Gary Peck for sharing your, ah hmm, 70+ years of family memories and photographs of times gone by at the lake. How blessed are we that six generations of family have enjoyed this peaceful retreat!

Research in old books and folders was required to find the public records to accurately trace the chain of custody of the lake's owners. Additional research was needed to flesh out the details – not just the who but also the what, when, and why. We would like to extend our sincere appreciation to Janice Lynx from the West Shore Historical Society, Mary Staub from the Hanover Area Historical Society 's Yelland Research Library & Archives, and Blair Williams from the Cumberland County Historical Society. Although your research may not have yielded the exact results we were seeking, your invaluable assistance guided us away from dead ends and toward the path of research success. We particularly thank the York History Center, especially Adam Bentz and Nicole Smith, and the staff at the York County Recorder of Deeds and Tax Assessment offices who not only tolerated our newbie questions, but took the time to teach us how to use their research tools and often pointed us in different directions to locate data which played an integral role in completing the larger puzzle. Your support and guidance were instrumental in our research journey.

We are immensely grateful to Ken Boyer, our local resident expert on the waterfowl and raptors of Silver Lake. Ken's generous contributions, including his exceptional photos graciously provided with permission, have added depth and richness to this project (© Ken Boyer; all rights reserved). His dedication to the preservation and dissemination of knowledge about the natural world is truly commendable. Thank you, Ken, for your invaluable support and for playing an integral role in bringing this book to fruition.

To Lewisberry's own Robert Griffith and Frank Grumbine for their patient sharing of their extensive knowledge and resources, you have made invaluable contributions. Kathy A. Weems, Art Williams, John R. Miller, and Jeri L. Jones – thank you for your knowledge, help and encouragement.

Despite all the assistance, knowledge gaps persist. Perhaps this knowledge is lost to the ages. Or perhaps it awaits another to find it. We have made every effort to faithfully present Silver Lake's story; any mistakes are all ours and not those of our amazing family, friends, and mentors above.

In conclusion, we want to express our heartfelt thanks to everyone who contributed to this project. Your support, whether through sharing memories, offering expertise, or providing valuable resources, has been instrumental in bringing this story to life. We are deeply grateful for your generosity, which has enriched our journey and made this endeavor possible. Together, we have documented the rich history of Silver Lake through its first 250 years, and we are profoundly thankful for your part in this journey. We look forward to sharing the story we have crafted with the world, knowing that it has been enriched by your kindness and generosity.

ABOUT THE AUTHORS

The Miller-Webb family ties to Silver Lake dates back over 80 years. It was the only property Bill and Florence Miller ever owned. Scott and Kathy's grandchildren are the sixth generation to enjoy the family's lakeside cottage, Linger Longer. While searching through old county records for a map, they stumbled across information that conflicted with the oral tradition known to current residents. Intrigued, they dug deeper and found that the oral histories were both wildly inaccurate and had gaping holes. This work is their effort to document and memorialize the history of Silver Lake for future generations. Along the journey, they realized that the history of Silver Lake itself is a microcosm for the settlement and evolution of York County, PA.

Scott and Kathy, both raised in Pennsylvania, worked most of their professional careers in the Washington, DC area and raised their children in Northern Virginia. Their cottage is and was the family gathering place where holidays, birthdays, and family events are celebrated with extended families – grandparents, aunts, uncles, and cousins. It is one constant in their family.

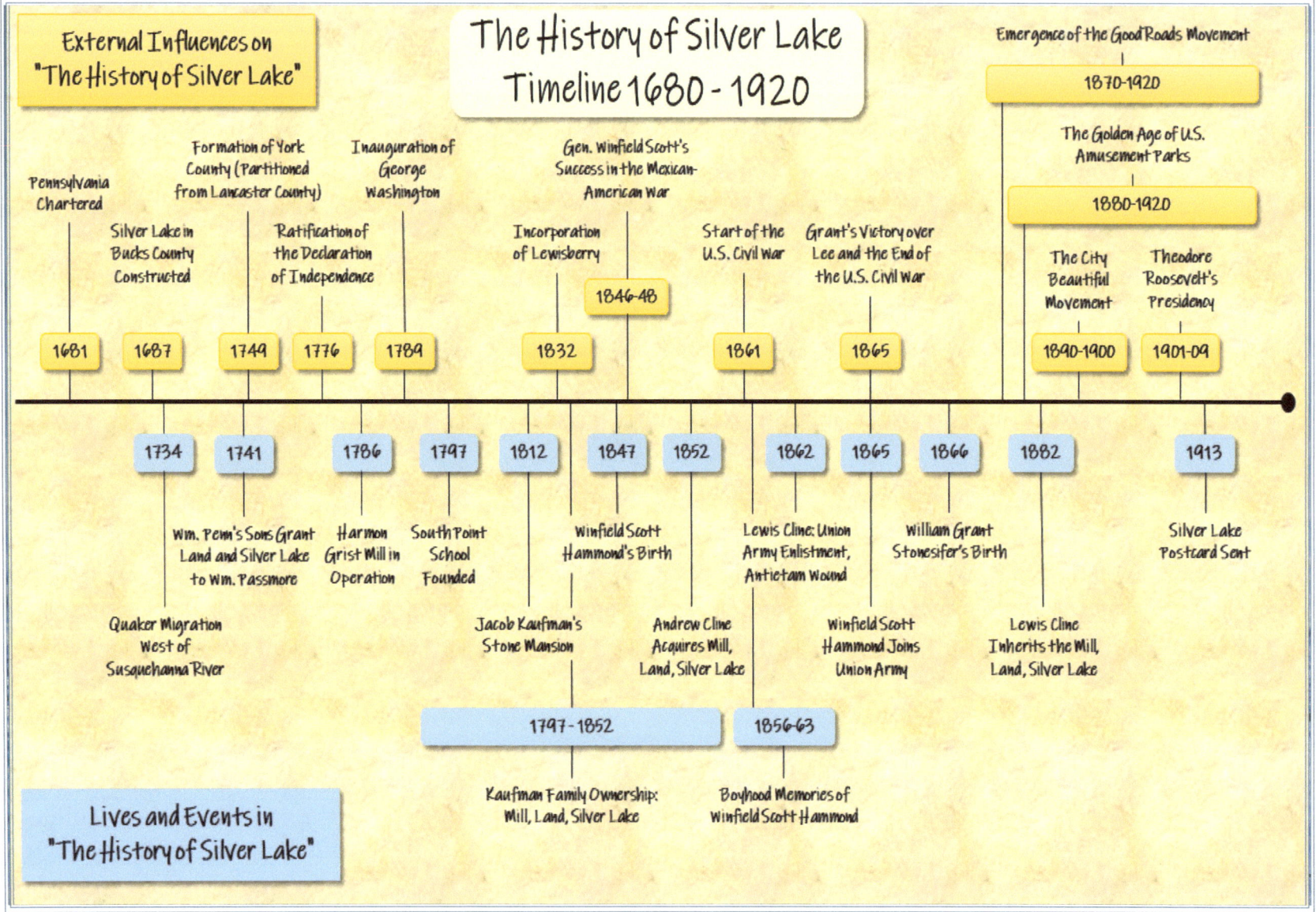

External Influences on
"The History of Silver Lake"

Emergence of the Good Roads Movement

1870-1920

The Golden Age of U.S. Amusement Parks

1880-1920

Pennsylvania Chartered

Formation of York County (Partitioned from Lancaster County)

Inauguration of George Washington

Gen. Winfield Scott's Success in the Mexican-American War

Silver Lake in Bucks County Constructed

Ratification of the Declaration of Independence

Incorporation of Lewisberry

Start of the U.S. Civil War

Grant's Victory over Lee and the End of the U.S. Civil War

The City Beautiful Movement

Theodore Roosevelt's Presidency

1846-48

| 1681 | 1687 | 1749 | 1776 | 1789 | 1832 | 1861 | 1865 | 1890-1900 | 1901-09 |

| 1734 | 1741 | 1786 | 1797 | 1812 | 1847 | 1852 | 1862 | 1865 | 1866 | 1882 | 1913 |

Wm. Penn's Sons Grant Land and Silver Lake to Wm. Passmore

Harmon Grist Mill in Operation

South Point School Founded

Winfield Scott Hammond's Birth

Lewis Cline: Union Army Enlistment, Antietam Wound

William Grant Stonesifer's Birth

Silver Lake Postcard Sent

Quaker Migration West of Susquehanna River

Jacob Kaufman's Stone Mansion

Andrew Cline Acquires Mill, Land, Silver Lake

Winfield Scott Hammond Joins Union Army

Lewis Cline Inherits the Mill, Land, Silver Lake

1797 - 1852

1856-63

Kaufman Family Ownership: Mill, Land, Silver Lake

Boyhood Memories of Winfield Scott Hammond

Lives and Events in
"The History of Silver Lake"

The History of Silver Lake Timeline 1920 - Today

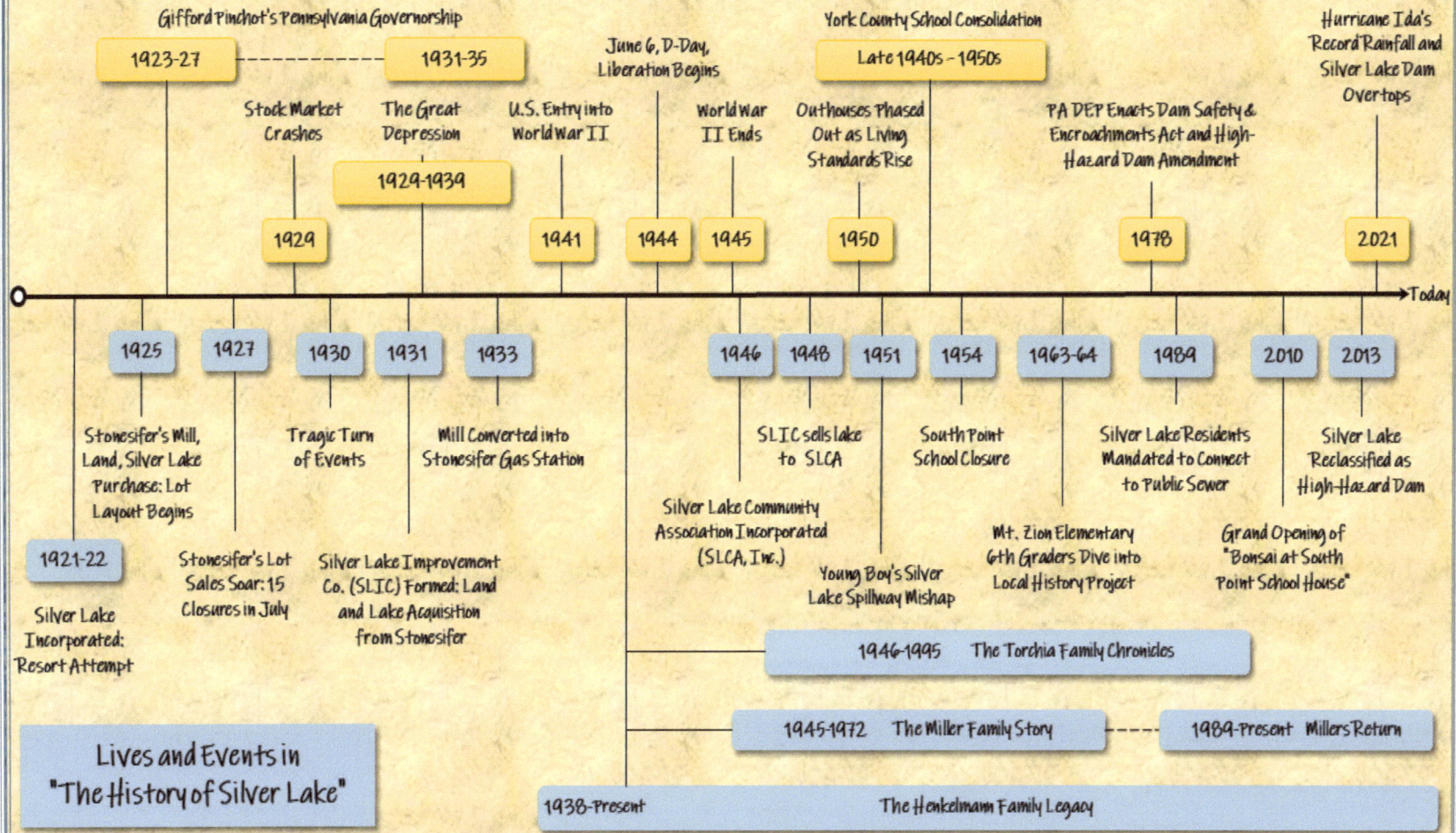

Gifford Pinchot's Pennsylvania Governorship

1923-27 — **1931-35**

Stock Market Crashes

The Great Depression

U.S. Entry into World War II

June 6, D-Day, Liberation Begins

World War II Ends

York County School Consolidation
Late 1940s – 1950s

Outhouses Phased Out as Living Standards Rise

PA DEP Enacts Dam Safety & Encroachments Act and High-Hazard Dam Amendment

Hurricane Ida's Record Rainfall and Silver Lake Dam Overtops

1929

1929-1939

1941

1944

1945

1950

1978

2021

Today

1925 **1927** **1930** **1931** **1933** **1946** **1948** **1951** **1954** **1963-64** **1989** **2010** **2013**

Stonesifer's Mill, Land, Silver Lake Purchase: Lot Layout Begins

Tragic Turn of Events

Mill Converted into Stonesifer Gas Station

SLIC sells lake to SLCA

South Point School Closure

Silver Lake Residents Mandated to Connect to Public Sewer

Silver Lake Reclassified as High-Hazard Dam

Silver Lake Community Association Incorporated (SLCA, Inc.)

Young Boy's Silver Lake Spillway Mishap

Mt. Zion Elementary 6th Graders Dive into Local History Project

Grand Opening of "Bonsai at South Point School House"

1921-22

Silver Lake Incorporated: Resort Attempt

Stonesifer's Lot Sales Soar: 15 Closures in July

Silver Lake Improvement Co. (SLIC) Formed: Land and Lake Acquisition from Stonesifer

1946-1995 The Torchia Family Chronicles

1945-1972 The Miller Family Story — **1989-Present Millers Return**

1938-Present   The Henkelmann Family Legacy

RFFERENCES

1. Jones, J. L. (2011, May). Geology of the western portion of York County Pennsylvania (York County Parks Geology Guide No. 10). Retrieved 2023, November 29, from URL: https://jonesgeo.com/wp-content/uploads/2022/06/Geology-of-the-western-portion-of-York-County-Pennsylvania-Part-1.pdf.

2. Pennsylvania Department of Conservation and Natural Resources. (2008). Pennsylvania Geological Survey: Map 13 - Gettysburg-Newark Lowland Section [Map]. Retrieved 2023, November 29 from URL https://www.nrc.gov/docs/ML0828/ML082880546.pdf.

3. Jones, J. L. (2023, August 16). Re: Request for geological info on Silver Lake in Lewisberry [Email to S. Webb].

4. United States Geological Survey. (2023). XY Location -76.870804, 40.136166 [Excerpt]. US Topo Map. Retrieved November 29, 2023 from URL: https://apps.nationalmap.gov/downloader/#/maps.

5. Gibson, J. (Ed.). (1886). History of York County, Pennsylvania (p. 630). F. A. Battey Publishing Co. History.

6. Gibson, J. (Ed.). (1886). History of York County, Pennsylvania (p. 630). F. A. Battey Publishing Co. History

7. Broersma, Luke, "Quakers, Sawmills and the Founding Father of Goldsboro". Retrieved 2024, Jan 6 from URL https://goldsborohistory.com/isaac-frazer-goldsboro-founding-father/.

8. Rudisill, J. (1991). York Since 1741. York Graphic Services.

9. Sholder, Kevin L, "Genealogical Intersection" Retrieved 2023, April 23 from URL https://sites.rootsweb.com/~rdrunner/web_data/p5686.htm, Dayton, Ohio, 2020.

10. York County, Pennsylvania. (1781). Deed Book 2E:479. Harman Updegraff to John Harmon: Illustrating the Chain of Title of the Land Containing Silver Lake.

11. Voaden, G. (circa 1970). Kaufman / Cline Mill [Photograph]. By Permission (Fee Paid), York County History Center, York, PA.

12. York County, Pennsylvania, Deed Book 2T:30. Sale of John Harmon's land, mill, and lake to John Kaufman 1797.

13. York County, Pennsylvania, Deed Book 2W:24. Sale of John Kaufman land and mill to Jacob Kaufman 1811.

14. York County, Pennsylvania, Deed Book 3T:69. Sale of water rights from John Hart to John Hart Kaufman 1845.

15. York County, Pennsylvania, Deed Book 3W:374. John H. Kaufman land, mill and lake to Andrew Cline.

16. York County, Pennsylvania, Deed Book 25A:440. John H. Kaufman granting of Water Rights to Andrew Cline.

17. York County, Pennsylvania, Assessment Office File #27-7: [Survey of A. Cline land acquired by L. Cline].

18. Harrisburg Telegraph. (1917, February 3). p. 3. "Miss Avis Ann Cline Dies".

19. Voaden, G. (circa 1970). Jacob Kaufman mansion[Photograph]. By Permission (Fee Paid), York County History Center, York, PA.

20. 1900, 1910, 1920 US Federal Census, United States of America, Bureau of the Census. Washington, D.C.: National Archives and Records Administration.

21. Ancestry.com. (2020). "York County, Pennsylvania, Biographical History Index", Ancestry.com Publications, Provo, UT, 2020.

22. York County History Center. Circa 1910 Postcard of Silver Lake.

23. Griffith, R. (2023, September 11). Interview with Robert Griffith, Lewisberry borough historian [Interview]. Conducted by S. Webb and K. Webb.

24. Hugill, P. J. (1982). pgs., 327-349 "Good Roads and the Automobile in the United States 1880-1929". Geographical Review. Retrieved 2024, January 9, from URL https://www.researchgate.net/publication/277491527_Good_Roads_and_the_Automobile_in_the_United_States_1880-1929.

25. Wilson, W. H. (1989). The City Beautiful Movement. Baltimore: The Johns Hopkins University Press.

26. York Daily Record. (1922, January 21). p. 5. Plans Ordered for Silver Lake Building.

27. The York Dispatch. (1922, April 6). p. 20.

28. York County, Pennsylvania, Deed Book 231:420. Sale of Elmira Cline (widow of Lewis Cline) land, mill, and lake to William G Stonesifer.

29. York County, Pennsylvania, Deed Book 231:420. Sale of Elmira Cline (widow of Lewis Cline) land, mill, and lake to William G. Stonesifer.

30. York County, Pennsylvania. (Deed Book 9R:200; Deed Book 9T:348).

31. York County Pennsylvania, Deed Book 231:420. Sale of Elmira Cline (widow of Lewis Cline) land, mill, and lake to William G Stonesifer.

32. Sixth Grade Pupils, Mt. Zion Elementary School. (1964). A Brief History of Lewisberry, PA: As Told By Those Who Lived Here. (Edith Cline's contribution, p. 22). York County History Center, York, Pennsylvania.

33. Top Schools in the USA (2023, June 6) Retrieved December 12, 2023, from URL https://www.topschoolsintheusa.com/biglerville-pennsylvania-history-economy-and-politics/.

34. Wildasin, Doyle F, History and Genealogy of the Stonesifer Family of Maryland and Pennsylvania, Hanover, Pennsylvania, 1983.

35. York County, Pennsylvania, Assessment Office File #27-7. Supplemental Survey of Silver Lake by W.K. Crowden.

36. US Federal Census, Year: 1930; Census Place: Fairview, York, Pennsylvania; Page: 1A; Enumeration District: 0019.

37. York Daily Record. (1928, May 12). p. 8. "Buys Mill from Father".

38. The York Dispatch. (1929, May 21). p. 4. Lewisberry News.

39. Harrisburg Telegraph. (1928, July 9). p. 6. Guy Stonesifer Builds 13th Cottage.

40. York County, Pennsylvania, Deed Book 250:518. Agreement between L.C. Stonesifer and Vacuum Oil Company, Inc.

41. York County, Pennsylvania, Deed Book 26I:472.

42. York Daily Record. (1935, February 26). p. 14.

43. York County, Pennsylvania, Deed Book 24Y:548. Silver Lake Improvement Company Certificate of Incorporation granted by Gifford Pinchot Governor.

44. York County, Pennsylvania, Deed Book 24Z:692. William G. Stonesifer sale to Silver Lake Improvement Company.

45. The York Dispatch. (1946 September 24). p. 14.

46. The York Dispatch. (1948, July 21). Dissolution Notice, p. 18.

47. York County, Pennsylvania (1946). Misc Instruments 31U:194. Certified 1946, January 28.

48. Law Insider. (n.d.). Legal definition of the term "Summer Colony". Retrieved 2023, October 23, from URL from https://www.lawinsider.com/dictionary/summer-colony.

49. York County, Pennsylvania, Deed Book 33Q:511. Sale of Silver Lake Improvement Company land and lake to Silver Lake Community Association.

50. York County, Pennsylvania, Deed Book 33P:463. Silver Lake Community Association Quit Clam to property owners.

51. The York Dispatch (1939, June 23) p.27. The York Dispatch (1939, August 05) p.12, Harrisburg Telegraph (1929, May 1) p.20, The York Dispatch (1934, June 8) p.27.

52. The York Dispatch. (1957, September 28). p. 6. "Suit File: Dispute over Mill Race to be Aired in Court".

53. The York Dispatch. (1971, April 6). p.8.

54. York Daily Record. (1977, January 17). p.6.

55. The York Dispatch. (1971, August 3). p. 37.

56. The York Dispatch. (1921, December 17). p.3. Silver Lake Lewisberry to be Made into Amusement Park.

57. The York Dispatch. (1922, January 30). p. 11. Salesmen for the Silver Lake Incorporated [Advertisement].

58. Harrisburg Telegraph. (1922, February 10). p.21. Announcement of Investors [Advertisement].

59. The York Dispatch. (1922, February 22). p.4. Promotion on the Sale of Stock [Advertisement].

60. The York Dispatch. (1922, April 6). p. 20.

61. The York Dispatch. (1920, May 28). p.11. Rendezvous – Atlantic City's New Park [Advertisement].

62. Wardle, L. (2016, December 2). More defunct and abandoned amusement parks across Pennsylvania [Photograph of Farquhar Park Pool]. PennLive. https://www.pennlive.com/entertainment/2016/12/defunct_amusement_parks_pa.html Accessed 2023, November 8.

63. The York Dispatch. (1920, January 31). p.6. "Citizens of 13th Ward Approve Plan".

64. Musser, B. (2020, March 6). White Rose Amusement Park [Photograph]. Retro York. Facebook. Retrieved 2023, November 08, from URL https://www.facebook.com/groups/retroyork/permalink/2802890566463770/?mibextid=S66gvF.

65. The Evening News (Harrisburg, Pennsylvania), (1945, July 19). p. 5. "Brothers Meet in Europe."

66. Torchia, M. (2023, June 7 & 16). Interview with Michael Torchia. [Interview]. Conducted by S. Webb & K. Webb.

67. York County, Pennsylvania. (1946). Deed Book 32I:618 and 32I:620 (Silver Lake Improvement Company); (1945) Deed Book 31I:563 (M. Arbegast); (1949) Deed Book 34T:66 (E. Toomey); (1949). Deed Book 34Y:37 (C. Wentz).

68. Margot, L. (c.1971). Hand Drawn Map Illustrating Torchia Hill [Map]. Personal Collection of Lee Margot.

69. The Gazette and Daily (York, Pennsylvania). (1955, October 13). p. 33. "Public Sale of Fairview Township School Property: Being Premises Known as South Point."

70. Torchia, M. (2023, June 16). Interview with Michael Torchia [Interview]. Conducted by S. Webb & K. Webb.

71. The State Museum of Pennsylvania. (n.d.). Quaker Mill House: Historic Pennsylvania Landmark. Retrieved 2023, November 29, from https://quakermillhouse.wordpress.com/colonial-country-home-landscape/triassic-brownstone/.

72. Williams, A. (2023, June 15). Re: Questions about the stones used around Silver Lake . [Email to S. Webb].

73. Pomeroy, Whitman and Co. (1876). Fairview Township map [Digital version]. By permission of York History Center, York, Pennsylvania.

74. South Edmonton Saga: Family history of Gottlieb Henkelmann & Wilhelmina Wentland, 1984, p. 563. South Edmonton Historical Society, Edmonton, Alberta, Canada.

75. Margot, L. (2023, June 12). Interview with Lee Margot on "The Henkelmann Story" [Interview]. Conducted by S. Webb & K. Webb.

76. York County, Pennsylvania. Deed Book 28G:160. Sale of Silver Lake Improvement Company land to Reinhold Henkelmann.

77. York County, Pennsylvania. Barnes, O. H. (1931). Plan of Lots "South Side of Silver Lake Fairview Township, York Co. Penna." [Recorded 1947, April 9]. [Portion of the plot presented]. [Note: The direction "South" is incorrect; it should be "North"].

78. Henkelmann, Rev. D. (2023, August 10). The Early Years of the Henkelmanns at "Silver Lake", Lewisberry, Pennsylvania [Document sent by email]. Email to S. Webb sent by L. Margot on 2023, August 10.

79. York Daily Record. (1945, December 24). p.4. Says Vets Want Church to Take More Interest in Social Problems.

80. Lishman, W. (1996). Father Goose. Crown. ISBN 0-517-70182-0.

81. Boyer, K. (2000s). Waterfowl & Raptors that use Silver Lake, Lewisberry, Pennsylvania [General Reference Letter]. Last updated 2023, August 25.

82. Miller, R. (2023, August). Interview with Robert "Bob" Miller. [Interview]. Conducted by S. Webb & K. Webb.

83. Miller Sistek, D. (2023, June). Interview with Donna Miller Sistek. [Interview]. Conducted by S. Webb & K. Webb.

84. Webb, S. (2023, June). K. Kunkle holding a silver-blue ball of bentonite clay from her private collection [Photograph].

85. Williams, A. (2023, June 18). Re: Silver-blue clay at Silver Lake [Email to S. Webb].

86. Jones, J. L. (2023, December 29). Re: Request for Review: Silver Lake History – Introduction, Geological Features, and References [Email to S. Webb].

87. Stonesifer, R. (n.d.). Delaware Family Genealogies. Retrieved 2023, November 18, from URL http://www.rstonesifer.com/genealogy/.

88. Travis, M. (2023, July 25). What to know about Michigan's deepest, largest and best inland lakes. Detroit Free Press. Retrieved 2023, November 18, from URL https://www.freep.com/story/news/local/michigan/2023/07/25/inland-lakes-in-michigan/70458593007/.

89. Silver Lake 2021 Spillway Inspection Photo. [Photograph]. Retrieved via Silver Lake Community Association Member FOIA request of the PA DEP.

90. Torchia, H. A. (2023, August). Interview with H. Andrew Torchia. [Interview]. Conducted by S. Webb & K. Webb.

91. Sixth Grade Pupils, Mt. Zion Elementary School. (1964). A Brief History of Lewisberry, PA: As Told By Those Who Lived Here. York County History Center, York, Pennsylvania.

92. Inglewood, M. (1924). Then and Now – Boyhood Adventures in Old Lewisberry. The Patriot. Harrisburg, Pennsylvania, as cited in Mt. Zion Elementary School's Sixth Grade Pupils' "A Brief History of Lewisberry PA. As Told By Those Who Lived Here." York County Historical Society, York, Pennsylvania (1964).

93. Pennsylvania Civil War Volunteers Biography. W.S. Hammond. Retrieved 2023, October 18, from URL http://www.pacivilwar.com/bios/hammond_winfield.php.

94. Prowell, G. R. (1907). History of York County Pennsylvania. J.H. Beers & Co.: Chicago. p. 890.

95. Altoona Tribune. (1933, January 20). p. 1. Death of W. Scott Hammond "Last Veteran Dies."

96. Ancestry.com. (2016, March 12). W.S. Hammond as identified by Harry E. Hammond; W.S. Hammond's first cousin three times removed. Retrieved January 12, 2024, from URL https://www.researchgate.net/publication/277491527_Good_Roads_and_the_Automobile_in_the_United_States_1880-1929.

97. Cocklin Funeral Home. (2020). Obituary of Donald Eugene Snelbaker (November 27, 1927 ~ October 24, 2020) [Obituary]. Cocklin Funeral Home. Retrieved 2023, November 21, from URL: https://www.cocklinfuneralhome.com/obituary/Donald-Snelbaker.

98. Weems, K. (2023). Lewisberry Historical Artifacts from the Personal Collection of Kathy A. Weems [Artifacts].

99. Mt. Zion Elementary School's Sixth Grade Pupils. (1964). A Brief History of Lewisberry, Pennsylvania, As Told by Those Who Lived   Here. York County History Center, York, Pennsylvania.

100.   Torchia, H. A. (2023, August). Interview with H. Andrew Torchia. [Interview]. Conducted by S. Webb & K. Webb.

101.   Forgas, B. (2023, September). Interview with Barbara Gross Forgas [Interview]. Conducted by S. Webb & K. Webb.

102.   Jennings, S. (2011, September 13). "The Zen Growth". The Daily News, p. 7.

103.   Lange, B. (2009, December). All Star: Ruth Stonesifer. Suburbanlife. Retrieved 2023, September 07, from URL https:// www.suburbanlifemagazine.com/article/158/All-Star-Ruth-Stonesifer#:~:text=As%20president%20of%2Gold%20Star,the%2Council%20of%20National%20Defenses.

104. Pennsylvania Volunteers of the Civil War Biography of Lewis Cline, Pennsylvania Soldier of the Civil War." (n.d.). Retrieved 2023, December 20, from URL http://www.pacivilwar.com/bios/cline_lewis.php.

105. York Daily Record. (1947, May 20). p. 12. "Miss Edith Cline, Lewisberry, Dies".

106. The Gazette and Daily (York, Pennsylvania). (1940, January 19). p. 14. "Anniversary Dinner Served at Lewisberry".

107. The Gazette and Daily York, Pennsylvania). (1936, September 15). p. 8. Mrs. Ivan C. Frey visit Cline home.

108. York County Archives. (1949, March 15). Inheritance Tax Forms. Copy provided on 2023, April 19. (fee required).

109. The Gazette and Daily (York, Pennsylvania) (1948, March 17). p. 4. Ivan C. Frey, Sr. Fatally Wounded.

110. The York Dispatch. (1913, May 26). p. 10. O H Barnes Injury at Brothers Ice Cream Shop.

111. News Comet (East Berline, Pennsylvania). (1948, August 13). p. 1. Dr. H.B. Hetrick, 81, dies.

112. The Gazette and Daily (York, Pennsylvania). (1952, December 5). p. 3. County doctor praised for service to others as final rites are held.

113. York County, Pennsylvania. Deed Book 260:134. G.H. Hetrick to H.C. Hetrick.

114. Historical Marker Database. (2018, February 3). Lewisberry, Pennsylvania Historical Marker [Photograph by William Fischer Jr.]. Retrieved December 21, 2023, from URL https://www.hmdb.org/m.asp?m=113712.

115. The Gazette and Daily (York, Pennsylvania) (1953, October 12). p. 3. "Plaque Dedicated to Late Lewisberry Physician".

116. York Daily Record. (2009, October 2). p.5. Dr. Eugene Hetrick's obituary.

117. Forgas, B. (2023, September). Interview with Barbara Gross Forgas [Interview]. Conducted by S. Webb & K. Webb.

118. Peck, G. (2023, December 18). Email exchange between Scott Webb and Gary W. Peck.

119. NavSource Online: Amphibious Photo Archive. (n.d.). Retrieved 2023, December 20, from URL https://www.navsource.org?archives/10/18/180037.htm.

120. York Daily. (1911, April 7). p.10. One Man Killed and Others Hurt in Cave-in at Dillsburg.

121. Milton Hershey School. (1945). Hershey Industrial School Yearbook (1945). Hershey, Pennsylvania.

122. New Jersey State Archives. (n.a.). Marriage Indexes. Trenton, New Jersey: New Jersey State Archives. Index Type: Bride; Year Range: 1951; Surname Range: A - K. [Bride's surname is "Good"].

123. Stonesifer Teasley, J. (2023, November 18). Text exchanges between Scott Webb and Jillian Stonesifer Teasley.

To learn more about the making of this remarkable book or to place an order for more copies, please visit our website at www.HistoryOfSilverLake.com or scan the QR code below.

If you have any inquiries, feel free to email us at info@HistoryOfSilverLake.com. Discounted pricing is available for purchasing multiple copies of the book for your organization, school, book club, or store.

www.ingramcontent.com/pod-product-compliance
Lightning Source LLC
Chambersburg PA
CBHW041551030426

42335CB00005B/188